W9-AAE-599

THE CHILDREN'S ATLAS OF

Natural
Wonders

THE CHILDREN'S ATLAS OF

Natural
Wonders

JOYCE POPE

The Millbrook Press
Brookfield, Ct

A QUARTO BOOK

First published in the United States of America in 1995 by
Millbrook Press, Inc.
2 Old New Milford Road, Brookfield, Connecticut 06804

Copyright © 1995 Quarto Children's Books Ltd

All rights reserved. No part of this publication may be reproduced, stored in a retrieval system
or transmitted in any form or by any means, electronic, mechanical, photocopying, recording
or otherwise, without the permission of the copyright holder.

Library of Congress Cataloging-in-Publication Data

Pope, Joyce.
The children's atlas of natural wonders / Joyce Pope.
p. cm.
"Designed and produced by Quarto Children's Books Ltd. ... London.
... First published in the United States of America ..."–CIP t.p.
verso.
"A Quarto book"–CIP t.p. verso.
Includes glossary and index.
Audience: Children in grades 2-6
Summary: A geographical atlas that explores the world's most
magnificent natural features.
ISBN 1-56294-886-5 (trade ed.), ISBN 1-56294-564-5 (lib. ed.), ISBN 0-7613-1001-0 (club ed.)
1. Physical geography–Maps for children. 2. Geology–Maps for
children. [1. Physical geography. 2. Geology.]
G1046.C1P6 1995 <G&M>
910' .02'0223–dc20

95-11778
CIP
MAP AC

This book was designed and produced by Quarto Children's Books Ltd,
The Fitzpatrick Building, 188 – 194 York Way, London N7 9QP

Creative Director Louise Jervis
Art Editor Nigel Bradley
Editor Samantha Hilton

Project editor Helen Varley
Designer David Goodman
Design Assistance Kim Musselle
Picture Manager Sarah Risley

Illustrations by Julian Baker (geology),
Josephine Martin/*Garden Studio,* Wildlife Art Agency

Quarto would like to thank the following
for providing photograph and for granting permission to reproduce copyright material. While every effort has been made to trace and acknowledge all copyright
holders, we would like to apologize for any omissions.

*(*b = *bottom,* c = *center,* l = *left,* r = *right,* t = top
TCL = Telegraph Colour Library*)*

Title page: *TCL;10* Michael Melford/*Colorific!; 11t & cl* Michael J. Howell/*Colorific!;*
cr David A. Ponton/*TCL; b* Sue Davies/*Life File; 12-13* Joanne McCarthy/*Image Bank; 12b* Eric Popple/*Life File; 14-15* Richard Lee Kaylin/*TCL; 15b* V.C.L./*TCL; 16-17*
Tom Mackie; *18-19* James Balog/ *Black Star*/*Colorific!; 18bl* Alon Reininger/*Contact Press*/*Colorific!; 19br* G.S.F.; *20-1* L.L.T. Rhodes/*TCL; 22-3* Benelux Press/*ACE; 23*
Bill Bachman/*ACE; 24-5* James Sugar/*Black Star*/*Colorific!; 24b* Enrico Ferorelli/ *Colorific!; 26-7t* Farrell Grehan/*Wheeler Pic*/*Colorific!; 26b* F.P.G./*L. Aiuppy*/*TCL; 27r*
G.S.F.; *28-9* Masterfile/*TCL; 29b* V.C.L./*TCL; 30b* Maja Koene/*Colorific!; 31t* Colin Monteath/*Mountain Camera; c* Andrew Ward/*Life File; b* Planet Earth/*Richard*
Matthews/*TCL; 32-3* L.L.T. Rhodes/*TCL; 33t* GAD/*TCL; 34-5* V.C.L./*TCL; 33b* Hans Hansen/ *Image Bank; 36-7* A. Warren/*TCL; 38-9* Juan Silva/*Image Bank; 39*
Hamish McInnes; *40-41* Patrick Morrow/*Black Star*/*Colorific!; 41* Olaf Soot/*Black Star*/*Colorific!; 42* D. Pratz/*TCL; 43t* G.S.F.; *c* V.C.L./*TCL; b* G.S.F.; *44* G.S.F.; *45*
G.S.F.; *46* Paul Slaughter/*Image Bank; 46-7* Mauritius/*ACE; 48b* G.S.F.; *48-49t* Geoff Smyth/*ACE; b* Fraser Ralston/ *Life File; 50t* Haugelo Castrillon/*Black*
Star/*Colorific!; b* Martin Page/*ACE; 51t* F.P.G./*J. Kugler*/*TCL; b* G.S.F.; *52b* John Moss/*Colorific!; 52-3t* Marcus Brooke/*Colorific!; b* Peter Adams/*ACE; 53b* Steve
Satushek/*Image Bank; 54l* T. Middleton/*TCL; 54-5* Marcus Brooke/*Colorific!; 55b* Jonathan Blair/*Black Star*/*Colorific!; 56t* Emil Schulthess/*Black Star*/*Colorific!; b* Space
Frontiers/*TCL; 56-7* G.S.F.; *58-9* Bob Thomason/*Colorific!; 58b* Mauritius/*ACE; 59b* Maja Koene/*Colorific!; 60b* Neil Folberg/*Image Bank; 60-61* Richard Nowitz/*Black*
Star/*Colorific!; 62-3* Alexander Stewart/*Image Bank; 62b* Terence Spencer/*Colorific!; 64* Peter Adams/*ACE; 65t* Planet Earth/*Jonathan Scott*/ *TCL; c* Heimo
Aga/*Colorific! b* John Cleare/ *Mountain Camera; 66b* D. Stewart/*TCL; 66-7* Sylvain Grandadan/ *Colorific!; 67b* Mark Stevenson/*ACE; 68* Mauritius/*ACE; 68-9t* R. del
Vecchio/*TCL; b* Mauritius/*ACE; 70* Marcus Brooke/*Colorific!; 71* John Hawkins/*Colorific!; 72-3* John Cleare; *74l* John Banagan/*Image Bank, r* Steel Photography/*ACE;*
75t Baron Sakiya/*Contact Press*/*Colorific!; b* Ralph & Daphne Keller/ *NHPA; 76-7t* Dave Saunders; *76c* Auschromes/*ACE; b* Patrick Ward/*Colorific!; 78-9* Lionel
IsySchwart/*Image Bank; 78b* Penny Tweedie/*Colorific!; 79* V.C.L./*TCL; 80bl* Robbi Newman/*Image Bank; 80tl* Rolf Richardson/*ACE; 80-1b* V.C.L./*TCL; 82-3t* Marcus
Brooke/*Colorific!; b* P&M Walton/*ACE; 84-5t* Ken Sakamoto/*Black Star*/*Colorific!; 84c* Stephen Wilkes/*Image Bank;* Andy & Karen Lacy/ *TCL]; 85* Ronald Toms/*ACE;*
88-9 Bryan & Cherry Alexander/*Colorific!; 90-1t* Colin Monteath/*Mountain Camera.*

Typeset In House
Manufactured by Bright Arts (Pte) Ltd, Singapore
Printed by Star Standard Industries (Pte) Ltd, Singapore

Contents

The Moving Earth

THE PLANET EARTH is never still. As it makes its yearly journey around the sun, it spins on its axis (an imaginary line from the North Pole, through the Earth, to the South Pole). There is movement in the air, which we feel as wind, and movement in the currents and tides of the seas and oceans, which we feel and see. Even the land is moving, although it feels solid and still.

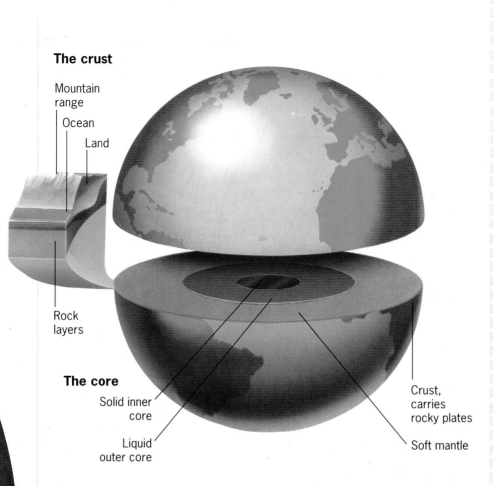

The crust

Mountain range

Ocean

Land

Rock layers

The core

Solid inner core

Liquid outer core

Crust, carries rocky plates

Soft mantle

The Earth's core

The Earth is not a completely solid ball. It is divided into layers. At its center is a solid core of iron and nickel, but surrounding it is a layer of iron and nickel so hot that it is molten ("molten" means "melted").

Iron and nickel melt at temperatures far higher than the boiling point of water. Such high temperatures mean that the outer part of the Earth's core is constantly moving about due to convection ("convection" is the name for the movement of heat in liquids).

The Earth's molten core is surrounded by a layer called the "mantle." It is made of stony minerals called silicates. The mantle is partly solid and partly molten and soft.

The Earth's crust

The outer layer of the Earth is called the crust. It ranges from 16 to 56 miles (25 to 90 kilometers) thick. But in some places, such as Yellowstone National Park, it is only 2 miles (3 kilometers) thin. The land we live on – the continental landmasses – is part of the Earth's crust. The remainder of the crust forms the floor of the oceans.

Even the Earth's crust moves. The continents consist of great plates of rock, which lie on the soft, upper layer of the mantle. They are not fixed, but slide slowly on the underlying layer of slush.

Supercontinents

Geologists believe that all the land on the Earth once formed one great supercontinent. They call it Pangea, meaning "All Earth." About 180 million years ago, movements inside the Earth caused Pangea to break up. The northern continental landmasses – North America, Greenland, Europe, and Asia – formed as Laurasia, the northern part of Pangea, broke up.

The southern part of Pangea, called "Gondwana," or "the land of Gond," broke up into the southern continents: South America, Africa, and Australia/Antarctica. About 50 million years ago, Australia broke away from Antarctica and began drifting southward.

180 million years ago: the super-continent Pangea, begins to break up

165 million years ago: Laurasia and Gondwana move apart

50 million years ago: the continents drift to their present positions

Present day

▲ *Mitre Peak in New Zealand, an example of a "young" mountain.*

Moving continents

The movement of the continents around the Earth is so slow that it is hardly detectable. Yet by studying places such as East Africa's Great Rift Valley, geologists can see that continents are still changing. Earthquakes along the San Andreas Fault in California, are evidence that the plates on which they lie are sliding past each other, carrying whole regions of land. The Himalayas in Asia are proof that continents are still colliding with such force that huge mountain ranges are being pushed up.

Sea floor is widening at mid-oceanic ridge

Oceanic plate slides beneath continent

Continental plate

Magma erupts from underground, forming volcanoes

▲ *When two plates meet, one slides beneath the other. Volcanoes and earthquakes on the Pacific Ocean's west and north rim mark the meeting of the Pacific, Eurasian, and Indian plates.*

A NEVER-ENDING STORY

The face of the Earth is constantly changing, but very slowly. It has taken 180 million years for the present seven continents to form from a single supercontinent.

Changing landscapes

The land is also formed and worn down by other, faster movements. We can sometimes see how the actions of volcanoes and storms, sun and ice, wind and water change the land's surface. And we can see their effects clearly. This book is about the natural wonders of our world – the result of all these different movements in and on the Earth.

Oceans

A visitor from outer space would see the Earth as a watery planet, for the oceans cover more than two-thirds of its surface.

In tropical areas, the surface of the ocean may be warm, but it cools quickly with depth, so overall there is little difference in temperature. We think of the sea as being a place of great movement , but the strong waves and currents are all at the surface. Below about 100 feet (30 meters), only the slow deep currents can be felt. Most oceans are dark, cold, still and seasonless.

In spite of this the oceans are rich in life. The first living things developed in ancient shallow seas. Today, the surface waters contain a great variety of living things, while the depths are home to some of the strangest living creatures. Beyond this, the oceans affect land life , for almost all of the water that falls as rain comes originally from the sea. The edges of the land are also warmed in winter and cooled in summer by the presence of the nearby oceans.

THE WORLD WITHOUT WATER

Beneath the seas are landscapes as varied as on any continent. Beneath the Atlantic Ocean, the mid-Atlantic Ridge marks the line where the North American, Eurasian, and African plates are tearing apart. Magma from deep in the Earth erupted onto the sea floor, forming volcanoes, the undersea mountains.

Atlantic Ocean

North America

Eurasian plate

North American plate

Mid-Atlantic Ridge

South American plate

South America

African plate

Africa

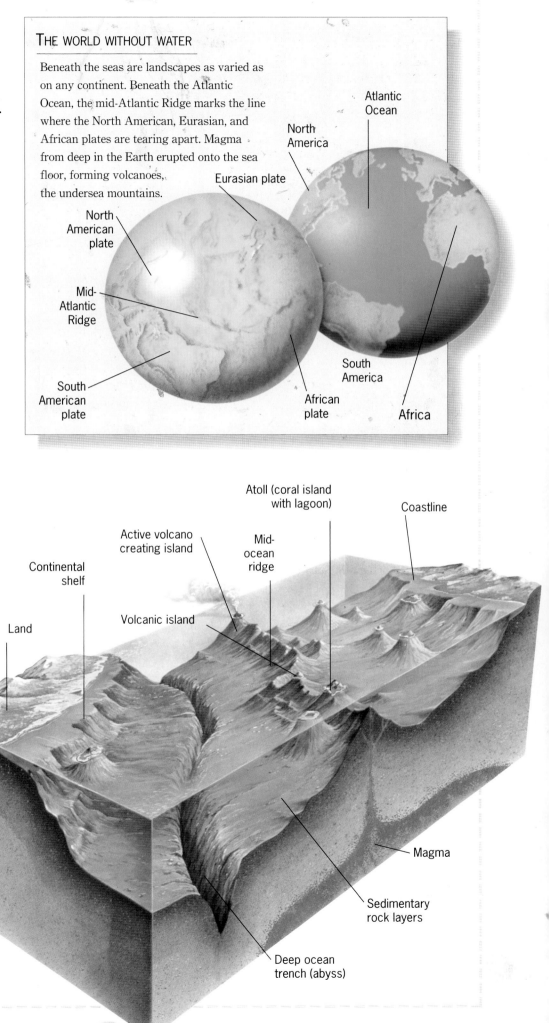

Atoll (coral island with lagoon)

Coastline

Active volcano creating island

Mid-ocean ridge

Continental shelf

Land

Volcanic island

Magma

Sedimentary rock layers

Deep ocean trench (abyss)

THE UNDERSEA LANDSCAPE

The edges of the continents slope down to the ocean floors. These are not flat, featureless, plains. They are scored with long trenches, miles deep, and ridged with ranges and chains of mountains. In places, volcanoes sometimes erupt lava onto the sea bed. Repeated lava flows from these "seamounts" may rise to the ocean surface, forming new islands. Chains of mountains running down the middle of the oceans mark the edges of the plates on which the continents float. The mountains are volcanoes and the lava they erupt is creating new land. Deep trenches occur where two plates meet, and one is being pushed beneath another.

NORTH AND CENTRAL AMERICA

NORTH AMERICA is the third biggest continent after Asia and Africa. Canada, in the north, has a cold climate, and nearby Greenland (Kalaallit Nunaat) is almost buried beneath 11,000 feet (3,350 meters) of ice. But Mexico, Florida, the West Indies, and Central America are in the tropics.

New meets old

Geologists discovered the oldest rocks on Earth in the ancient "shield" region of central Canada. A computer worked out that they are 3,962 million years old. Of North America's many mountain ranges, the Rockies and other west coast ranges are the youngest. The huge American and Pacific continental plates meet along North America's west coast. The region is dotted with active volcanoes, and earthquakes occur from California, all along this unstable coastline.

Over in the east, between New York and Florida, the mountain ranges were formed when the American continental plate collided with the Eurasian plate. That was more than 400 million years ago.

Ice covered the north of North America from about 2 million to 10,000 years ago. When the ice melted, the meltwater made a huge lake around the edge. The Great Lakes between Canada and the U.S. are the remains of it. Today, Lake Superior is still North America's biggest freshwater lake. Northern Canada and Alaska, in the Arctic Circle, are still ice-covered for most of the year.

Cowboy country

In the middle of the U.S. there are dry deserts, with the dramatic rock landscapes and steep river canyons you see on cowboy films. Great, slow rivers like the Mississippi flow across the central plains southward to the sea, spreading the mud and sand they carry in times of flood, making new land.

▼ *Central America is a region of volcanic mountains, with tropical rainforests in the coastal lowlands.*

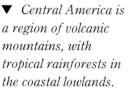

ALASKA • Mt. McKinley

DENALI NATIONAL PARK *p24–25*

Pacific Ocean

Rocky Mountains

N O

CRATER LAKE *p16–17*

YELLOWSTON *p26–27*

San Francisco □

CALIFORNIA

SAN ANDREAS FAULT *p18–19*

BRYCE CANYON *p14–15*

Los Angeles □

GRAND CANYO *p12–13*

MEXI

◀ *Most of North America's high peaks are in the chains of western mountains, such as the Rocky Mountains, shown here in Colorado.*

▼ *The "buttes" (flat-topped hills) of hard rock in Monument Valley on the Utah/ Arizona border tower above a desert of softer rocks. This has been the location of many western movies.*

FACTS ABOUT NORTH AMERICA

♦ North and Central America cover about 9,420,000 square miles (24,400,000 square kilometers), 16 percent of the world's land.

♦ The northernmost point on the mainland of North America is over 70°N. The southern border is south of Mexico at 15°N.

♦ The westernmost point is in Alaska at about 170°W. The most easterly point is in Newfoundland, Canada, at 52°30'E.

♦ Central America covers about 200,000 square miles (517,980 square kilometers).

♦ Mount McKinley, Alaska, is the highest peak, 20,320 feet (6,193 meters) above sea level.

NEWFOUNDLAND

ANADA

Lake Superior
GREAT LAKES

NIAGARA FALLS *p28–29*

Atlantic Ocean

FLORIDA

EVERGLADES *p22–23*

WEST INDIES

Caribbean Sea

NTRAL
ERICA

Panama
Canal

PANAMA

▲ *Tundra vegetation covers north Alaska. The summer temperature is rarely above 50°F (10°C), and the subsoil is permanently frozen.*

▶ *Swamps cover large areas of Florida, the state in the far south- east of the U.S. Most of southern Florida is just above sea level.*

GRAND CANYON

The PLATEAU OF NORTHWEST ARIZONA is split by a gash in the rocks 280 miles (445 kilometers) long. This is the Grand Canyon. It was cut by the rushing waters of the Colorado River. Standing on the edge of this split in the desert floor, visitors marvel at the huge vistas across walls falling to the river in steep steps, and at the amazing colors of the rocks.

The width of the Canyon varies from 4-15 miles (6.4-24 kilometers). Erosion has widened it faster than the river has deepened it. As the river cut down, the sun, wind, and winter frost wore away the sedimentary rocks it exposed. It quickly cut through softer rocks, forming steep cliffs. But hard rocks erode more slowly. They remain as wide ledges jutting out from the walls. If you travel from top to bottom of the Canyon, the layers of rocks you pass tell you much of the story of the Earth's formation.

At its deepest, the Canyon measures 1 mile (1.5 kilometers) from rim to river. Its depth is due to great mountain-building forces which are pushing the whole area up. In the last 5 million years, the Colorado Plateau has risen more than 4,000 feet (1,219 meters). It is still rising.

And, flowing at an average 12,200 cubic feet (346 cubic meters) per second, carrying millions of tons of grit and pebbles torn from its bed, the Colorado River is still, like a giant file, carving the Grand Canyon across the plateaus of the southwest U.S.

▼ *Tourists explore the calmer stretches of the Colorado River in inflatable rafts.*

WILDLIFE OF THE GRAND CANYON

In the Canyon's warm interior live desert plants and animals – like the datil yucca and the Grand Canyon rattlesnake. Higher up, the climate is cooler and the plants and animals are like those found from the Great Lakes to British Columbia, such as the Arizona gray fox. In the cool forests of the Northern Rim, 9,000 feet (2,700 meters) above sea level, live northern species, such as the chipmunk.

Grand Canyon rattlesnake

Datil yucca

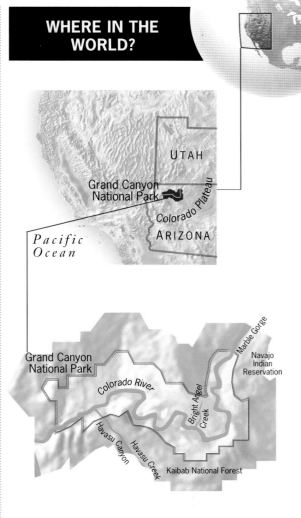

▲ *The steep sides of the Grand Canyon are a breathtaking sight. They are striped with reddish and yellowy shales, brown mudstone and silts, tan-coloured sandstone, and gray, pink, and purple limestone. They seem to change color with the sunlight and clouds.*

◆ The Grand Canyon of the Colorado River runs through northwest Arizona. The river flows west through the Grand Canyon, then turns south.

◆ The rocks of the Grand Canyon were formed under a sea that covered Arizona from about 2 billion to 250 million years ago. About 6 million years ago, volcanoes erupting nearby added cinder cones, lava falls, and basalt flows to the western end of the Canyon. The Colorado River may only have started cutting the Grand Canyon about 2 million years ago.

◆ The height of the Grand Canyon's rim rocks is between 6,000 and 8,500 feet (1,829 and 2,590 meters) above sea level.

◆ Several creeks in adjoining canyons, such as Bright Angel Creek and Kaibab Creek, flow into the Colorado River.

STORY OF THE ROCKS

At the bottom of the Grand Canyon's Inner Gorge are some of the world's oldest rocks – formed about 2,000 million years ago. Above them, each layer is younger. The rim rocks are about 225 million years old. Younger rocks which once lay above them have worn away.

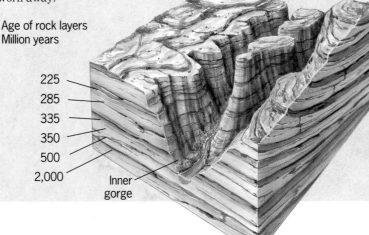

Age of rock layers
Million years

225
285
335
350
500
2,000

Inner gorge

BRYCE CANYON

THERE ARE THOUSANDS of canyons in the Bryce Canyon National Park. The Park gets its name from a settler called Ebenezer Bryce. He arrived in 1875 to cut timber from the forests of the Paunsaugunt Plateau surrounding the canyons. The canyon behind his house was called Bryce Canyon, and later this name was given to the whole area.

The canyons are all clustered in what looks like a bowl dug out of the floor of the plain. You can stand at an observation point on the edge of the plateau, and look down into the canyons in this bowl of desert wilderness.

Each canyon is guarded by high rock walls. At the top they break up into fantastically shaped pinnacles, called hoodoos. The rocks of this amazing place are made of brilliant red and orange sandstone. They are formed from sediments, which were deposited by streams and rivers about 60 million years ago. Iron in the sediments produces the rich red colors in the rocks today – the more iron, the redder the rock.

▶ *The hoodoos tower over the canyons. They seem to change shape and color in the light and shadow at different times of the day and year.*

Many of the hoodoos have names. The Paiute Indians, who used to live in the area, called them "Red Rocks Standing Like Men." Modern travelers have named some of the smaller canyons – one is called "Fairyland Canyon." Some of the hoodoos have also been named – one is called "Thors Hammer."

Bald eagle

Prickly pear cactus

WILDLIFE OF THE NATIONAL PARK

The Utah prairie dog, found only in southern Utah, is the rarest of the many animals native to Bryce Canyon National Park. Black bears and cougars are the largest, and the bald eagle is one of the largest birds. A colorful flower is the prickly pear cactus. The forests are of spruce, fir, and aspen trees. Bristlecone pines – the Park's longest-living trees – grow at higher altitudes. Some may be 4,000 years old.

Blue spruce

HOW THE HOODOOS WERE SCULPTED

Bryce Canyon's rocks were formed from silts left by an ancient sea. Much later, faults (breaks) developed, and a huge block of land was pushed above sea level. Rivers carved canyons through the rock. Then the weather ate away the soft rock and carved the hard rock into pinnacles.

Original rock

Rivers carve channels through rock

Wind and ice sculpt rocks into pinnacles called hoodoos

WHERE IN THE WORLD?

NEVADA UTAH

Bryce Canyon National Park

Shakespear Point

Paria River

Thors Hammer

Fairyland Canyon

Paunsaugunt Plateau

Bryce Canyon

Bryce Creek

Rainbow Point

♦ Bryce Canyon National Park is in southwest Utah.

♦ The area was declared a national park in 1928.

♦ It is about 22 miles (35 kilometers) from north to south and covers 57 square miles (145 square kilometers).

♦ The National Park averages about 8,000 feet (2,400 meters) above sea level, but it slopes slightly from south to north. Rainbow Point, near the southern end, is more than 9,000 feet (2,740 meters) high, and Shakespear Point, in the north, is less than 8,000 feet (2,400 meters) above sea level.

♦ Energetic travelers may walk on more than 50 miles (80 kilometers) of trails in the canyons to see the hoodoos close to.

▶ *Thors Hammer*

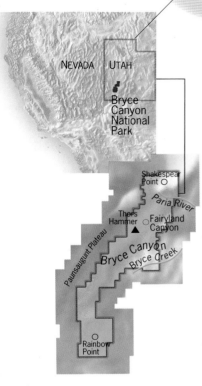

CRATER LAKE

THE HIGH peaks of Oregon's Cascade Range surround Crater Lake, the deepest lake in the U.S. Evergreen forests sweep around its circular shore. But what fascinates everyone about this lake is its intense blue color.

Today, the lake's surface is still and peaceful. But thousands of years ago it formed in the crater of a huge volcano called Mount Mazama. After the last eruptions had ceased, about 7,000 years ago, the volcano's immense crater began to fill with water. After 1,000 years, its depth had reached 1,932 feet (590 meters).

No streams flow into Crater Lake. Summer rains and winter snows filled the crater with water and still keep its water level constant. The water is so unpolluted and crystal clear that the light reaches 725 feet (220 meters) beneath the surface. As the light penetrates the water, the colors in its spectrum are absorbed one by one, starting with the long red wavelengths. By the time the light has traveled 725 feet (220 meters) through the water, only the short wavelengths, blue and violet, remain to be reflected. They give the lake its intense blue color.

Mount Mazama has been a sacred place for Native Americans since it first erupted. Its serene crater lake was scarcely disturbed by humans until gold prospectors discovered it in the 1850s. Only half a century later, in 1902, its wilderness was preserved as America's sixth National Park.

WILDLIFE OF MOUNT MAZAMA

Birds, squirrels, and pine martens live in the evergreen forests that surround the sacred lake. Wildflowers, like the Indian paintbrush, grow among the trees. No fish are native to the lake, but trout and salmon. introduced by the settlers have survived there.

Steller's jay

Common monkeyflower

▲ Volcano-shaped Wizard Island in the center of the beautiful blue Crater Lake is indeed a volcano. It resulted from a minor eruption that took place long ago through a vent (lava channel) in Mount Mazama's crater.

♦ Crater Lake is in the Cascade Range in southern Oregon.

♦ The lake is 1,932 feet (589 meters) deep.

♦ The crater walls rise about 2,000 feet (609 meters) above the lake surface.

♦ Although it is in an area of very cold winters, Crater Lake does not freeze. Geologists think this is because volcanic activity warms the depths of the lake.

♦ The eruption of Mount Mazama was 60 times as big as the eruption of Mount St. Helens in Washington State, in 1980.

♦ Mount Scott, a volcanic mountain nearby, rises to a height of 8,926 feet (2,721 meters).

THE VOLCANO'S STORY

About 7,000 years ago, small earthquakes warned that a new volcano might erupt. Underground, trapped gases expanded. When they reached the surface, they threw ash and lava 20-30 miles (32-48 kilometers) high. Ash covered the ground as far as Canada 700 miles (1,126 kilometers) away. Ash beds 60 feet (18 meters) thick still surround the crater rim. In time, more than 13 cubic miles (53 cubic kilometers) of lava jetted from the volcano, filling valleys 300 feet (91 meters) deep. This flow so weakened the volcano's cone that its walls collapsed inward. They filled the magma chamber and left a huge crater. During the next 1,000 years, rain and snow filled the crater with water.

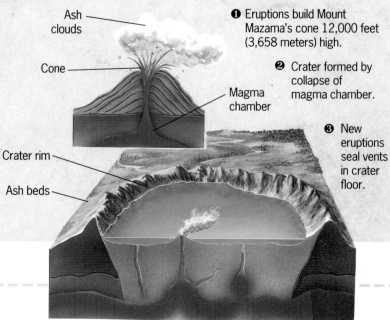

Ash clouds

Cone

Magma chamber

Crater rim

Ash beds

❶ Eruptions build Mount Mazama's cone 12,000 feet (3,658 meters) high.

❷ Crater formed by collapse of magma chamber.

❸ New eruptions seal vents in crater floor.

THE SAN ANDREAS FAULT

People living in western California are used to earthquakes. In 1906, San Francisco was almost destroyed by the region's severest earthquake this century. There have since been many minor tremors. San Francisco and the other cities of western California are built on or near the San Andreas Fault. This huge fault is the largest of many in the region. Earthquakes may happen along any of them.

A fault is a crack in the Earth's crust caused by pressure and movement of rocks. Some of the biggest faults are at the edges of the great plates that carry the continents. The San Andreas Fault runs along the margin between the North American Plate and the Pacific Plate, which stretches from California to Japan. About 600 miles (965 kilometers) of it run through southern California, and into the sea.

The Pacific Plate is moving northeast by about 2 inches (5 centimeters) a year. It does not move evenly, but sticks, then jerks, shaking and shattering the nearby rocks. This may be felt on the surface as earth tremors. If the movement is severe and nearby rocks are split, cracks appear in streets, and buildings may topple.

As the two plates have moved against each other, the rocks on either side of the San Andreas Fault near San Francisco have jammed together. Geologists predict that in the future they will jerk apart, causing another great earthquake like the one that caused such devastation in the city of San Francisco in 1906.

▼ *The San Andreas faultline looks from above like a huge ditch running across the western California countryside and into the sea.*

◄ *Earthquakes can cause the walls of houses to shift and collapse. In the California earthquake zone, buildings now have to be specially designed to withstand frequent shocks.*

CALIFORNIA QUAKES

The Pacific plate carries a tiny piece of the U.S. For 30 million years it has been moving part of California past the North American plate toward Alaska at an average 2 inches (5 centimeters) a year. But the plates move unevenly. They become locked, and a build-up of tension causes them to jerk apart. During the California 1989 earthquake, the Pacific plate slipped 6 feet (1.8 meters) past the North American plate. At the same time, it rose about 3 feet (91 centimeters) higher.

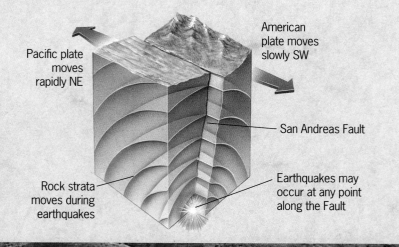

Pacific plate moves rapidly NE

American plate moves slowly SW

San Andreas Fault

Rock strata moves during earthquakes

Earthquakes may occur at any point along the Fault

▲ On April 18, 1906, the ground beneath San Francisco shook, and great cracks appeared in the streets. This picture shows Union Street after the earthquake.

Point Reyes

San Francisco

Sierra Nevada

San Andreas Fault

CALIFORNIA

Los Angeles

Pacific Ocean

Gulf of California

LOWER CALIFORNIA

♦ The San Andreas Fault is more than 600 miles (965 kilometers) long. It originates beneath the Gulf of California, turns west toward Los Angeles, and runs north to San Francisco, through Point Reyes into the sea.

♦ Rocks in Point Reyes, California, have moved 310 miles (498 kilometers) in about 10 million years. They match rocks in the Tehachapi Mountains in the south.

♦ Recent earthquakes, like the 1994 Los Angeles earthquake, were caused by small faults at an angle to the San Andreas Fault. Geologists predict a second great earthquake, perhaps near San Francisco.

▼ This picture shows close up a crack that appeared in the ground after a recent earthquake in the San Andreas Fault.

CARLSBAD CAVERNS

EVERY EVENING, as night falls, bats in their thousands stream across part of the New Mexico desert, near the Texas border. They are off on an insect-hunting flight.

This amazing sight intrigued the area's settlers in the 1800s. They explored canyons and ridges to find where the bats came from. Their curiosity led them to a huge natural amphitheater in the Chihuahuan Desert of the Guadalupe Mountains. Here they found the entrance to the Carlsbad Caverns.

The Caverns form a vast network of underground caves, tunnels, and chambers covering 73 square miles (189 square kilometers), and descending more than 1,000 feet (305 meters). Some caverns are gigantic. One, called "The Big Room," rises to 255 feet (78 meters) at its highest point.

Over hundreds of thousands of years, rainwater containing dissolved minerals has seeped into the caverns and has hardened into strange forms – huge columns, delicate spires, and strange, twisted formations looking like stone plants. These limestone decorations, created by mineral-laden water, make many of the caverns look like the underground palaces of fairytale kings and queens.

▲ *The Mexican free-tail bat is the most prevalent of the seven or more types of bats that roost in the Bat Cave. Its name describes its thin, dangling tail. The bats sleep hanging upside-down in the caves during the day. At night they hunt flying insects and other prey.*

▲ *Over millions of years, water containing dissolved limestone dripped slowly from the cavern ceilings and hardened into stalactites. Drops that fell to the ground grew into stalagmites.*

Pacific Ocean

NEW MEXICO

Guadalupe Mountains

Carlsbad Caverns National Park

El Paso   Chihuahuan Desert

TEXAS

Gulf of Mexico

♦ The Carlsbad Caverns are in southeast New Mexico, near the Texas border. The entrance is 4,400 feet (1,341 meters) above sea level.

♦ More than 20 miles (32 kilometers) of underground tunnels and caverns have been explored down to 1,000 feet (305 meters), but there is much more to discover.

♦ Many caves have been given names, like "The King's Palace" and "The Queen's Chamber." "The Iceberg" is a giant boulder. The biggest stalactite, called "The Giant Dome," is 20 feet (6 meters) in diameter.

♦ In the Chihuahuan Desert, temperatures may be below freezing in winter, or above 100°F (38°C) in summer. Yet outside temperatures do not reach far into the caverns, which are a constant 56°F (13°C).

♦ The Caverns were declared a National Park in May, 1930.

WATER SCULPTURES

The Carlsbad Caverns began as deposits laid down under a sea 200 million years ago. About 65 million years ago, earth movements lifted the sea floor, making the rocks crack. Rainwater, made acid by carbon dioxide absorbed from the air, seeped into the cracks, and ate the surrounding limestone rock away. In time, the acid ate passages and caverns out of the rock. For over 3 million years, the mineral-laden water dripped through the cavern ceilings onto walls and floors, and hardened into beautiful formations.

Mineral-laden water drips through ceilings, hardens into stalactites and stalagmites

Acid water eats into limestone, forming caves

Limestone rock

THE EVERGLADES

APART OF NORTH AMERICA that is half land, half sea, is the region called the Everglades at the tip of southern Florida. It is a region of lagoons, grassy swamps, and wooded islands. South Florida was covered by the sea until recent geological time. The land rose out of the sea only between 8,000 and 6,000 years ago. Even now it is very low-lying. Its average height above sea level is only 8 feet (2.4 meters).

Native Americans called the Everglades "grassy river," yet you see little open water. The heavy summer rains that fall on southern Florida create a 50-mile (80-kilometer) wide river – but it is invisible because it is covered almost everywhere by a sea of high sawgrass.

Since the 1930s, more and more of the water that has fed the Everglades has been diverted to towns, factories, and farms. In the 1980s, the government set up water conservation schemes. Plants have been built to desalinate (remove the salt from) seawater to provide fresh water. But conservationists think too little has been done too late, and that by the year 2000, much of the Everglades will have dried out completely.

EVERGLADES WILDLIFE

The Everglades is a unique habitat for wetland wildlife. Freshwater species include native fish, such as the Florida gar, and water birds, such as the Everglades kite. Like many freshwater species, the wood stork nests in the dry season. The brown pelican, the loggerhead turtle, and the manatee, a huge mammal, live in salt water, but come into the rivers.

Manatee

Wood stork

▲ *Alligators lurk in the sawgrass in the freshwater areas of the Everglades.*

◄ *Mangrove trees live on the seawater side of the Everglades. They have roots that can live underwater, and aerial shoots through which they breathe.*

WHERE IN THE WORLD?

♦ The Everglades are in South Florida. They cover an area of about 4,000 square miles (10,360 square kilometers). The Everglades National Park is 1,563 square miles (4,047 square kilometres) in area.

♦ In a few places, rocks jut through the sea of sawgrass to form small hills, called "hammocks." These stand out like tropical islands, covered with dense forests of slash pine and royal palm.

♦ The Everglades are shrinking because huge towns, such as Miami, have grown up along the coast of Florida. Miami's population grows at the rate of 900 people a day.

▼ *The National Park was created in 1947 to protect the Everglades' plant and animal life.*

EVERGLADES FRESHWATER CYCLE

About 60 inches (150 centimeters) of rain falls on the Everglades each year. The Kissimmee River, to the north, floods during the heavy summer rains. The water collects in wide, shallow Lake Okeechobee to the south. From there, it soaks into the spongy soil, and, like a great slow-moving river without banks, seeps southward to the Gulf of Mexico at the rate of about 100 feet (30 meters) a day.

The arrows on the map show the direction of flow of freshwater from northern Florida to Lake Okeechobee, and southward through the Everglades to the surrounding seas.

DENALI NATIONAL PARK

THE HIGHEST mountain in North America is in the north. Towering over 7,000 feet (2,000 meters) above the peaks of the Alaska Range is Mount McKinley. It is more than 20,320 feet (6,194 meters) high.

The history of Mount McKinley starts with the huge Denali Fault, which runs across Alaska from the border with Canada to Bristol Bay. A fault is a split that occurs when tensions in the Earth cause rocks to move in relation to each other.

About 60 million years ago, the Denali Fault tore open, releasing huge amounts of lava, which flowed over the countryside. Volcanoes threw more lava and ash on to the surface, and this hardened into new rocks. The pressures caused by this volcanic activity made the land buckle and fold. The mountains of the Alaska Range were pushed up along the fault line.

Meanwhile, some magma had remained deep in the Earth's crust. Slowly it cooled and hardened. Then it was pushed up to form Mount McKinley as it is today.

In 1917, a national park was created in the area around Mount McKinley. In 1980 the area of the park was enlarged to 6 million acres (2,428,000 hectares) — bigger than Massachusetts. It was called Denali National Park and State Preserve. The native Athabascan peoples named North America's highest mountain Denali. The word means "The Great One."

HOW A GLACIER FORMS

A glacier begins when snow collects in a hollow, or "cirque," high on a mountain slope. The weight of more snow falling on top of it changes the snow to ice. When the ice has become 110 feet (38 meters) or more deep, it cracks away from the cirque's back wall, and begins to flow slowly downhill. When a glacier melts, it dumps all the rocks it carries. These form piles called moraines.

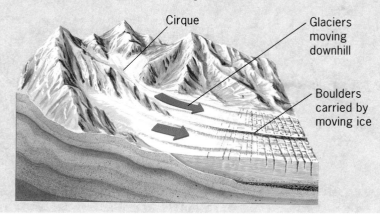

Cirque

Glaciers moving downhill

Boulders carried by moving ice

◀ *In the last 2 million years, glaciers have carved the flanks of the Alaska Range. Some still survive on the freezing higher peaks.*

▲ *Mount McKinley is so high, the summit is often completely hidden in cloud and can only be seen on a rare clear day.*

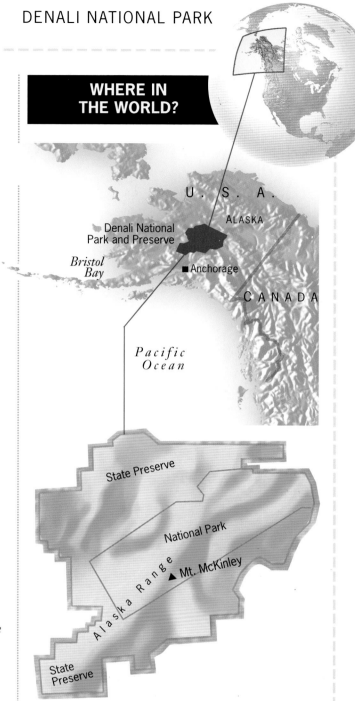

U. S. A.

ALASKA

Denali National
Park and Preserve

*Bristol
Bay*

■Anchorage

C A N A D A

*Pacific
Ocean*

State Preserve

National Park

Alaska Range ▲ Mt. McKinley

State
Preserve

◆ Mount McKinley is in the Alaska Range in central Alaska, 200 miles (322 kilometers) south of the Arctic Circle. It was named after Senator, later President, McKinley.

◆ The peaks of the Alaska Range average 13,000 feet (4,000 meters) above sea level. Trees grow up to 2,700 feet (800 meters).

◆ A thermometer left on Mount McKinley at 15,000 feet (4,572 meters) was found 15 years later. It registered -97°F (-72°C), the lowest North American temperature recorded.

◆ The National Park preserves more than 37 mammal species, 139 bird species, and 430 species of flowering plants.

WILDLIFE OF DENALI

Mount McKinley National Park was created in 1917 to preserve grizzly bears, wolves, and caribou for hunters. But Denali is rich in all types of wildlife. It provides nesting grounds for polar birds, such as Arctic terns, jaegars, and ptarmigan. Miniature wildflowers grow in the high tundra, including the forget-me-not, the Alaska state flower.

Willow
ptarmigan

Forget-me-not

YELLOWSTONE NATIONAL PARK

WHEN PEOPLE FIRST BEGAN to visit Yellowstone's boiling springs, geysers throwing hot water high into the air, and bubbling mud pools, they called it "Wonderland." So stunning was its impact that in 1872 the American government made Yellowstone the first national park in America – and in the world.

Yellowstone is in a place where the Earth's rocky crust is very thin – a mere 2 miles (3 kilometers) from the zone of hot, molten (liquid) rocks in the Earth's interior. Most land surfaces are 15 to 30 miles (24 to 48 kilometers) thick. As a result, in places the ground at Yellowstone is warm to the touch, and earthquake tremors often occur.

The great earth movements that pushed up the Rocky Mountains caused much volcanic activity. Huge magma chambers formed beneath Yellowstone. About 2 million years ago, one of these was the center of a gigantic eruption. Then another eruption took place about 600,000 years ago. A caldera formed, thousands of feet deep and several miles across. And about 150,000 years ago, there was a third huge eruption in the West Thumb area of Yellowstone Lake.

So Yellowstone is a huge volcano cone that has been filled in by lava flows. They ended about 60,000 years ago, and glaciers began carving the landscape. But geologists think that one day, the Yellowstone scenery will be torn apart – by another great volcanic eruption.

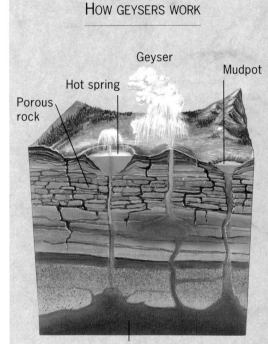

HOW GEYSERS WORK

Porous rock · Hot spring · Geyser · Mudpot

Molten (liquid) rock

Rainwater seeping through porous rock layers is heated underground and shoots to the surface as hot springs or fumaroles (steam jets). Some water is superheated under pressure and surfaces as geysers. Acid gases from fumaroles break down rocks into mud, which surfaces as mudpots and mud volcanoes.

WILDLIFE OF YELLOWSTONE

Yellowstone is a wonderful wilderness area roamed by moose and other deer, and by bison. There are black and brown bears in the mountains, and wolves are reappearing. Mountain whitefish and three subspecies of cutthroat trout bask in warm waters. They are preyed on by ospreys and other fishing birds. The fringed gentian is the park flower.

Fringed gentian

Osprey

Cutthroat trout

▶ *The landscape of Yellowstone National Park was created by glaciers and, after they melted, by rivers. The fast-flowing Yellowstone River is still at work, carving spectacular falls and gorges into its route through the park.*

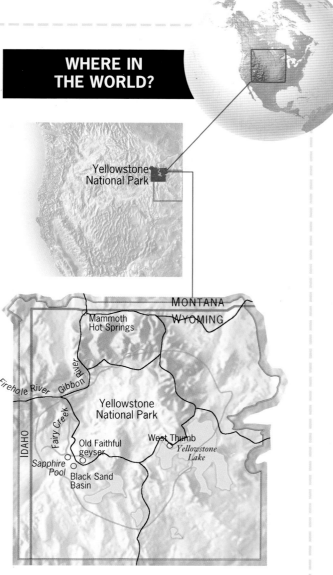

WHERE IN
THE WORLD?

MONTANA
WYOMING

Mammoth
Hot Springs

Firehole River

Gibbon River

Fairy Creek

Yellowstone
National Park

IDAHO

Old Faithful
geyser

West Thumb

*Yellowstone
Lake*

Sapphire
Pool

Black Sand
Basin

♦ The Yellowstone National Park, named after the Yellowstone River, is in northwest Wyoming.

♦ The park is 3,472 square miles (8,992 square kilometers) in area, and between 5,300 and 11,358 feet (1,615 and 3,462 meters) above sea level.

♦ Yellowstone Lake is 139 square miles (360 square kilometers) in area.

▲ *More than 10,000 geysers and steam jets (called "fumaroles"), brightly colored hot springs, and other thermal features make Yellowstone the largest geyser park.*

▶ *A mudpot releases gas through hot mud.*

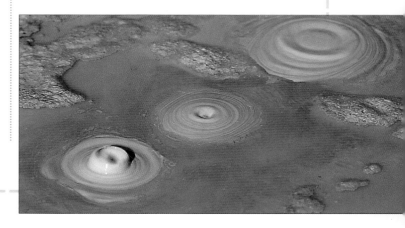

THE NIAGARA FALLS

THE NIAGARA RIVER is only 35 miles (56 kilometers) long, but it is one of the most famous rivers. Halfway along its course, it pours all the water that overflows from four of the five Great Lakes over the Niagara Falls. You can hear the thunderous roar long before you see the falling water.

Altogether, 34 million gallons (155 million liters) of water drop 167 feet (51 meters) over the waterfall every minute of every day and night. They drop over a ledge of hard rock and flow into the Niagara Gorge. This leads into Lake Ontario, which is 326 feet (99 meters) lower than the other Great Lakes.

The rock over which the Falls drop is so hard that a small island of it resists the power of the water. It is called Goat Island, and it divides the Falls in two, either side of the Canada/U.S. frontier.

The Niagara Falls are geologically young. They date from about 10,000 years ago, after the end of the last Ice Age. Water from the melting ice caused Lake Erie to overflow. The floodwaters formed the Niagara River, which cut into its bed to form the Niagara Gorge on its northward flow.

Between the Falls and the Gorge, the Niagara River dashes through the spectacular Whirlpool Rapids, where the current rushes through rocks at over 30 miles (48 kilometers) an hour.

▶ *The Horseshoe Falls on the river's south (Canadian) side form a curve 2,200 feet (670 meters) long. The American Falls, on the north side, are 1,060 feet (323 meters) long, and straight. Boats take visitors in front of the Falls to see the cascading water.*

THE FATE OF THE FALLS

The Niagara Falls formed at an escarpment (a point where land drops steeply) much closer to Lake Ontario. The water flows over hard rock that resists its force, but it cuts through the softer rock beneath it, and pieces break off. In this way, Niagara Falls have retreated 7 miles (11 kilometers) from the escarpment. In the 1950s, geologists predicted that the Falls will gradually move back to Lake Erie. But engineers have strengthened the rock bed with rods and cables, slowing the erosion of the Falls to less than 2 inches (5 centimeters) a year. So the Falls may survive for thousands of years.

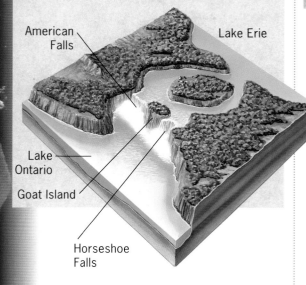

American Falls

Lake Erie

Lake Ontario

Goat Island

Horseshoe Falls

▼ *The Niagara Falls shimmer behind a mist of droplets thrown up by the force of the falling water.*

♦ The Niagara Falls are on the Niagara River, which connects Lake Erie with Lake Ontario and crosses the border between Canada and the U.S. The more northerly part of the Falls is in New York State, and the more southerly part is in Ontario, Canada.

♦ The Niagara Falls are among the largest and most impressive in the world. Their name, "Niagara," comes from the Native American name for the Falls, which is "Onguiaahra," meaning "thunderer of waters."

♦ About half the river's flow above the Falls has been diverted to generate hydro-electricity. At night, the Falls are illuminated for a few hours by electricity they generate.

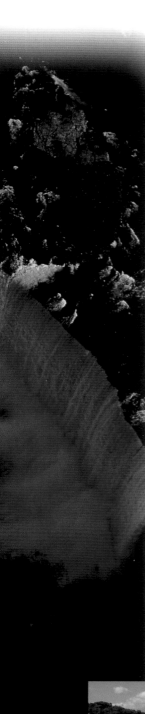

SOUTH AMERICA

FOR MUCH OF the last 100 million years, South America was not joined to Central America. It was an island continent, like Australia, floating in the southern ocean. Then, about 25 million years ago, Central America rose out of the sea to form a land bridge between North and South America.

Mountains and volcanoes

South America is different from the other continents that were once part of Gondwana, the ancient supercontinent, for it is mountainous. It has relics of ancient mountains in the east and south. Running along its western edge are the Andes, which include some of the highest peaks in the world.

The Andes are new fold mountains, like the North American Rockies. They were formed as the American continental plate, carrying most of South America west, collided with the Nasca plate beneath the Pacific Ocean, which is moving east. There are many volcanoes in the Andes, some recently extinct and some active. This, and many earthquakes in the region, indicate that the American plate is still moving away from Africa, and that this collision is still going on.

Some of the world's longest rivers drain the flanks of the Andes toward the Atlantic Ocean, more than 2,000 miles (3,000 kilometers) away. The Amazon and its many mighty tributary rivers flow through the remains of great tropical rainforests. Many previously unknown species have recently been discovered among the rich wildlife of the Amazon Basin.

◀ *Flat-topped mountains called "tepuis" rise above thick rainforest in the Guiana Highlands of northeastern South America.*

CENTRAL AMERICA

○ Guajira Peninsular

VENEZUELA

ANGEL FALL

Guiana Highlands

RORAIMA

COLOMBIA

River Amaz

Punta Parinas ○

A m a z o n
B a s i n

THE

M a t o G

S O U T H

LAKE TITICACA
p34–35

BOLIVIA

Atacama ○ Desert

CHILE

▲ Mt. Aconcagua

Pacific Ocean

TORRES
DEL PAINE *p*

Cape Horn ○

◄ *The Andes Mountains stretch all the way down South America's west coast. This photograph shows The Glaciers National Park at the southern tip of the Andes, a region of melting glaciers and fast-flowing rivers.*

Equator

BRAZIL

I C A

Cabo Branco

▲ *The Atacama Desert in Chile is one of the driest and least hospitable places on Earth.*

FACTS ABOUT SOUTH AMERICA

♦ South America is the fourth largest continent.

♦ This southern continent has an area of 6,874,600 square miles (17,805,200 square kilometers), and covers about 12 percent of the Earth's land surface.

♦ The continent stretches from about 12°N in the Guajira Peninsular, Colombia, to 56°S at Cape Horn, Chile, its most southerly point. Cabo Branco in Brazil is about 35°W and Punta Pariñas in Peru is 81°E.

♦ The tapering shape of South America gives it a very long coastline – 15,803 miles (25,432 kilometers) in total. This gives 1 mile (1.6 kilometers) of coast for every 435 square miles (1,127 square kilometers) of land.

♦ The Andes is a chain of high mountains running 5,500 miles (8,850 kilometers) down the continent's western edge. Many peaks are higher than 20,000 feet (6,000 meters). Mount Aconcagua at 22,834 feet (6,960 meters) is the highest peak in the southern hemisphere.

◄ *Amazonia is the largest remaining expanse of rainforest. It stretches from South America's northern coast to the Mato Grosso plateau in the south, and from the Andes in the west to the Atlantic Ocean.*

THE AMAZON

THE MIGHTY AMAZON is the world's largest river. It is almost 4,000 miles (6,437 kilometers) long – not quite as long as the Nile River in Africa, but it carries more water. At any time it is carrying about two-thirds of all the world's river water. Over 1,000 tributaries feed this huge river with water. Seventeen are more than 1,000 miles (1,600 kilometers) long. They drain nearly one-third of South America.

About 80 inches (200 centimeters) of rain falls a year over most of the Amazon basin. Near the equator, rain falls every day. Further north and south, it rains for about 200 days a year.

Each rainy season – from December to June – tributary streams empty their floodwaters into the western Amazon. The river overflows its banks and floods the rainforest. The floods bring nutrients to the land, and, for a season, increased living space for many creatures. Fishes and even dolphins swim among the trees.

More species of animals live in the Amazon forests than anywhere else in the world. The trees cast such dense shade that few plants grow on the forest floor. Creatures that can swim, climb, or live in the trees survive best.

▶ *For most of its length, the Amazon is a slow river. It headwaters (tributary streams) flow fast down the Andes' eastern slopes, but on average, the river descends about 1 inch (2.5 centimeters) for each 1 mile (1.5 kilometers) of its course.*

Capybara

Arrow poison frog

AMAZON WILDLIFE

The bouto, the Amazon dolphin, is one of many freshwater species native to the Amazon waters. Poison arrow frogs live near pools on the forest floor and in tree hollows. They have bright warning coloration. Capybaras live in groups beside rivers and lakes. They are the largest rodents, the size of a small pig. Hoatzin nest in trees above water at the swampy forest edges and eat green leaves.

Hoatzin

Bouto

◀ *The Amazon is home to about 9,000 species of insects, birds, and animals – almost half the total known to us. But the rainforest is being destroyed so quickly, it is feared that this great diversity may not last much longer.*

WHERE IN THE WORLD?

Pacific Ocean

Atlantic Ocean

COLOMBIA

ECUADOR

PERU

Iquitos ●

River Negro

Solimões River

River Amazon

● Manaus

Amazon Estuary

○ Marajo Island

A m a z o n B a s i n

Rondônia

Mato Grosso

BRAZIL

Andes Mountains

BOLIVIA

♦ The Amazon has the world's biggest river basin, extending across Brazil, into Peru, Colombia, and Bolivia. It drains an area of about 2,722,000 square miles (7,000,000 square kilometers) – nearly one-third of South America.

♦ The source of the Amazon is high in the Andes of Peru, more than 17,000 feet (5,000 meters) above sea level.

♦ Flooding during the rainy season raises the water level of the Solimões (the western Amazon above Manaus) by as much as 55 feet (17 meters).

♦ One of the Amazon's many tributaries, the Madeira River, is 2,100 miles (3,380 kilometers) long. It is the longest tributary river in the world.

MOUTHS OF THE AMAZON

In 1499, a Spanish captain sailing out of sight of the coast found his ship was in fresh waters. He sailed shoreward and his was the first European ship to anchor in the 150-mile (240-kilometer) wide Amazon estuary. More than 28 billion gallons (127 billion liters) of water a minute flow into the sea. They dilute its salinity (saltiness) for more than 100 miles (160 kilometers). They deposit a fan-shaped heap of silt on the ocean floor beyond the continental shelf. The mouth of the Amazon is a network of islands. The largest, Marajo Island, is the size of a small European country.

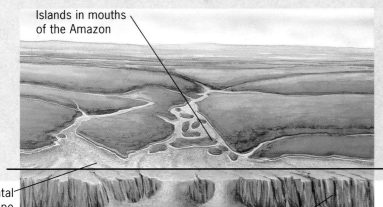

Islands in mouths of the Amazon

Continental slope

Fan-shaped sediments

Continental shelf

▶ *The tall forest trees are supported by wide bases with projections called "buttresses" all round.*

LAKE TITICACA

THE LARGEST upland lake in the world is Lake Titicaca, high in the Andes. It is 3,200 square miles (8,288 square kilometers) – so large that part of it is in Peru, and part is in Bolivia. The lake is on the Altiplano – a high plateau between the east and west Andes. On either side, peaks soar 20,000 feet (6,000 meters) high.

Lake Titicaca is 12,506 feet (3,812 meters) above sea level. It is large and deep enough for ships to sail on it, so it is the highest navigable lake in the world.

The waters of over 25 rivers drain into the lake but only one drains out of it. It is also fed by 22 inches (56 centimeters) of rain a year, and, in summer, by melted snow from the Andes. Because of this, the surface may rise by as much as 16 feet (4.9 meters) in the rainy season, between December and March. Strong winds and evaporation keep the water level stable. But sometimes the lake still mysteriously rises and falls.

Lake Titicaca was given its name by ancestors of the Indians who live on its shores. Its meaning is thought to be "Rock of the Puma" or "Crag of Lead." There are 41 islands in the lake. On some, archeologists have found ancient ruins, which show that the lake was the home of one of the earliest American civilizations.

▶ *For thousands of years, the native Uro Indians have lived on islands which they make from a reed they call "totora" that grows on the lakeside. They also use this reed to make boats for transportation.*

WILDLIFE OF THE HIGH ANDES

Killifish

Andean hillstar

Catfish and killifish (the *Orestias* species) live in Lake Titicaca. A native frog is *Telmatobius*, which grows up to 12 inches (30 centimeters) long. The Andean hillstar is a hummingbird of the high Andes.

▶ *Totora, a reed like a bullrush, and quinua, a plant that produces grain, are unique to Lake Titicaca.*

♦ Lake Titicaca straddles the border between Peru and Bolivia. It is on the Altiplano, the high plateau between the Cordillera Real range of the East Andes and the peaks of the West Andes overlooking the Pacific Ocean.

♦ This lake is the second largest in South America. Lake Maracaibo in Venezuela is the largest.

♦ The lake measures 120 miles (193 kilometers) from north to south. Its maximum width is about 45 miles (72.4 kilometers). At its deepest, it is about 900 feet (275 meters), but its depth varies – it is deepest on the Bolivian side.

♦ It is divided into two main parts, each with a different name. The smaller southeastern part is called Lago Uiñaimarca, and the larger northwestern part is called Lago Chucuito.

♦ The surface temperature of the lake averages 57°F (14°C).

♦ More than 25 rivers drain into Lake Titicaca.

♦ Medical research has shown that the Indians of the Altiplano have developed bigger hearts and lungs to enable them to live in the lower air pressure at such high altitudes.

HOW LAKE TITICACA WAS FORMED

Only the peaks of the Andes are snowcovered, but during the last Ice Age the snow came down to a much lower level. When it ended, about 10,000 years ago, the meltwater poured down the mountains to be trapped in a great valley on the Altiplano. This is how Lake Titicaca was formed.

Ten thousand years ago, Lake Titicaca was bigger than it is today. Geologists know this because they have found the remains of ancient beaches on mountain slopes above the lake. When they measured the distance from those beaches to the bottom of the lake, they found that the lake must have been at least 150 feet (45.7 meters) deeper than it is today.

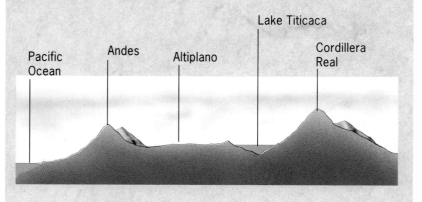

THE ANGEL FALLS

AROUND DEVIL MOUNTAIN in eastern Venezuela, the loud roar made by the Angel Falls can be heard for a long way across the rainforest. The Angel Falls is the world's highest waterfall. It is formed where the Churún River tips over a huge cliff and down the mountainside.

The water falls a total 3,212 feet (979 meters) – a drop 15 times higher than the Niagara Falls in North America. From the top of the Falls, the water cascades 2,648 feet (807 meters) down the cliff. Then it hits hard rock jutting out from the cliff, and drops 564 feet (171 meters) into a deep pool, called Angel Canyon, at the cliff foot.

The Angel Falls have nothing to do with angels. They are called after an American pilot, Jimmy Angel. In 1933 he flew over the flat-topped Devil Mountain, and recorded in his log book that he had seen the Falls. But he was not the person who discovered them – their existence was first made public in 1910 by a South American explorer.

The force of the Falls varies. The source of the Churún River is the rain that falls on Roraima's flat top. In the dry season between January and May, the water flow from the Churún River is often reduced to a trickle. The Angel Falls are at their most spectacular in the rains, between June and December.

The rainforest is so dense that flying over the Falls on an air excursion is still the best way to see them. In the rainy season, when the water level is high, visitors take boats along the Churún River to see them from below.

CASCADE FROM A CLIFF TOP

Churún River

Fissures in sandstone

First cascade

Second cascade

Amphi-theater eroded from rock

Churún River

Devil's Canyon

As they near the edge of Devil Mountain, some of the Churún River waters trickle through fissures in the mountain's ancient sandstone. They burst out of the rock below the lip of the precipice to join water falling over the cliff top. Behind the curtain of water, a huge amphitheater has been eroded. At the bottom, where they cascade into Devil's Canyon, the Angel Falls are 500 feet (152 meters) wide.

▲ *The spectacular Angel Falls, Devil Mountain, the Churún River, and the rainforest region around them are now preserved as Canaima National Park.*

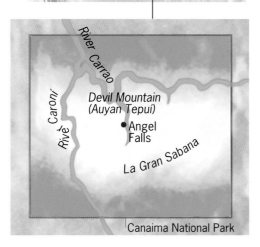

Ciudad Bolívar
Angel Falls
Guiana Highlands

V E N E Z U E L A

River Carrao

River Caroní

Devil Mountain (Auyan Tepuí)

● Angel Falls

La Gran Sabana

Canaima National Park

♦ The Angel Falls are in the Guiana Highlands in southeast Venezuela, about 160 miles (260 kilometers) southeast of Ciudad Bolívar.

♦ The Gran Sabana, the uplands drained by the Churún River, rise from 6,500 feet (1,980 meters) to 10,000 feet (3,000 meters). The Churún is a tributary of a river that flows north to join the great Orinoco River on its journey to the sea.

♦ Devil Mountain is a flat-topped mountain, called a "mesa" in Spanish. The Indians of the region call it a "tepuí" Their name for Devil Mountain is "Auyan Tepuí."

WILDLIFE OF THE RAINFOREST

Heliconid butterfly

Many rainforest trees are immensely tall and hung with creepers called "lianas." Orchids and ferns attach themselves to branches to be near the light. Many monkeys live in the tree canopy. Howling monkeys communicate over long distances by piercing calls. In the shade beneath the canopy, huge groups of Heliconid butterflies fly slowly. Nocturnal tapirs forage on the forest floor.

Tapir

RORAIMA

DEEP IN THE RAINFOREST of southern Venezuela is a strange, mountainous region called "La Gran Sabana," meaning "The Great Sheet." The name is a good description, because in this region cluster many flat-topped mountains called "tepuís" by the local Indians.

Tepuís are mountains with steep, high sides and broad, flat tops. Rainforest vegetation clings to their tops, tumbles down their sides, and arches across deep ravines between them. Highest and broadest of all the tepuís is Roraima. Its name means "Father of Waters," perhaps because many rivers cascade down its steep sides. Some flow north to join Venezuela's great Orinoco River. Others flow south to join the rivers feeding the thirsty Amazon.

So remote is La Gran Sabana and so thick is the rainforest that not until the last century did Europeans see Roraima. Towering above the forest, its top in cloud, with waterfalls glistening down its sides, it looked an amazing sight.

Roraima is a huge block of sandstone on a platform of volcanic rocks. It was formed under the sea about 300 million years ago – the ripple marks made by ancient waves are impressed in the stone. Many gullies and cracks are worn in the top, and these gradually widen and split. A huge boulder called the Towashing Pinnacle has broken away and lies at the foot of the main mountain block. Other pieces will break away, and so Roraima will be destroyed.

▲ *Roraima is still a beautiful sight – but it is no longer so remote as in 1884 when it was first climbed. The new Pan American Highway has made it easier for tourists to reach. Every year, local Indians guide many visitors to Roraima's once mysterious tabletop plateau.*

WILDLIFE OF THE LOST WORLD

Roraima hummingbird

In the 19th century, an English writer, Arthur Conan Doyle, wrote a tale called "The Lost World". It was about a group of explorers who climbed a mountain in the jungle and found dinosaurs and other prehistoric creatures living there. Arthur Conan Doyle was fascinated by reports of travelers who had seen Roraima, and he based his tale on this strange mountain. In 1884, when Roraima was climbed and the plateau on top was explored, zoologists found more than 50 different types of flowering plants, 120 animal species, tropical birds, such as honeycreepers, and some birds no one had ever seen before, like the Roraima coquette. But they found no "living fossils."

▶ *The thick rainforest of La Gran Sabana still conceals many mysterious tepuís, or flat-topped mountains, whose steep sides no human has yet climbed.*

VENEZUELA ●Ciudad Bolívar

Guiana Highlands

Mt. Roraima ▲

GUYANA

COLOMBIA

Roraima Indian Reservation

Pan-American Highway

BRAZIL

♦ La Gran Sabana is part of the Guiana Highlands in the southeast corner of Venezuela. Roraima is on its eastern border with Guyana and Brazil.

♦ Roraima is 9,219 feet (2,809 meters) above sea level. Its steep cliffs rise 4,000 feet (1,220 meters) above the plain. The plateau on top is about 25 square miles (40 square kilometers).

♦ Roraima is one of about 100 tepuís – table mountains – between Colombia in the west and the Guyana/Brazil border in the east. "Tepuí" is a Pemón Indian word meaning "mountain." Tepuís are called "mesas" by the Spanish-speaking South Americans, and "table mountains" in English.

♦ Until very recently it was almost impossible to reach La Gran Sabana by land. The first rough road was laid through the rainforest in 1973. By 1990 it had been paved. It is now Venezuela's most scenic modern road.

TORRES DEL PAINE

Near the tip of South America, the great rocky spires of the Torres del Paine range rise 8,500 feet (2,590 meters) above the grassy plains of the Magellanes region of southern Chile. Glimpsed through breaks in the clouds that often hide them, the peaks are astonishing. They are made of pink granite, and the summits are capped with black slate.

The Torres del Paine massif was formed millions of years ago by the forces that tore apart the southern supercontinent of Gondwana. Later, for many thousands of years, glaciers carved its peaks into fantastic shapes.

There are still seven glaciers in the valleys of the main massif, but they are all melting. Several lakes in the area that were scooped out by the ice, or dammed by moraines, show how far the glaciers once reached. In the last 90 years, nearly 1 mile (1.6 kilometers) of ice has retreated from just one valley. To the north, the Park merges into The Glaciers National Park of Argentina where the glaciers are not retreating.

The Torres del Paine National Park covers 700 square miles (1,814 square kilometers). To its early explorers, this wild region of fjords, mountains, windy plains, islands, and lagoons of the far south of Chile seemed the very end of the Earth. To the west are the icy seas of the Southern Ocean. To the east, low hills descend into dry grasslands. Torres del Paine, the most southerly national park, has some of the most varied scenery and vegetation of any national park in the world.

THE LONGEST MOUNTAIN CHAIN

The peaks of Torres del Paine lie on the eastern slope of the Andes. They are part of this great chain of mountains, which runs from Alaska, all the way south to Antarctica. Collisions between the American plate, moving westward, and the Pacific and Nasca plates, moving east, has pushed up these great chains of mountains.

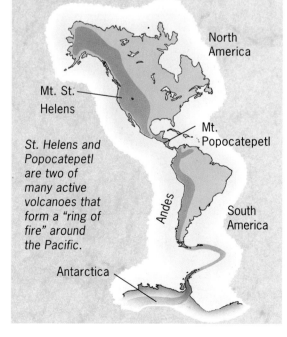

North America

Mt. St. Helens

Mt. Popocatepetl

St. Helens and Popocatepetl are two of many active volcanoes that form a "ring of fire" around the Pacific.

Andes

South America

Antarctica

▲ *"Torres del Paine" means "Towers of Paine" in Spanish. The name may describe these soaring peaks seen from a distance, for "payne" means "blue" in the local Indian language. But the mountains may have been named after a British woman called "Paine," who used to climb there.*

▶ *These pink granite spires in the Paine massif are the "Torres" or "Towers" of Paine, which give the range its name.*

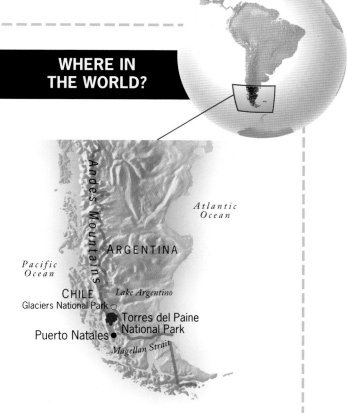

Andean
condor

Guanaco

WILDLIFE OF TORRES DEL PAINE

Torres del Paine became a national park in 1959. Sheep farmers had exploited the region, and destroyed many native animals. Guanacos (wild ancestors of the llama), and huemel deer, have recolonized. Cougars and the rare Geoffroy's cat are sometimes seen. Patagonian and Fuegan foxes compete with small skunks and hairy armadillos for fruit. The soaring Andean condor, and the Darwin's rhea – which cannot fly – are among many uncommon bird species.

♦ The Torres del Paine National Park is in the Magellanes region of southern Chile, close to the border with Argentina on the east. The Straits of Magellan lie a little to the south. The town of Puerto Natales is over 92 miles (150 kilometers) away.

♦ Attempts to preserve the area were begun in 1925, but the nucleus of the National Park was established in 1959. It was called the Lake Gray Tourism National Park. It has since been extended and there are plans to enlarge it even more. It may one day be merged with Argentina's The Glaciers National Park.

♦ More than 100 bird species have been recorded in the National Park, including many species of water birds. There are reptiles, amphibians and fishes, and more than 170 species of insects.

EUROPE

EUROPE IS THE SMALLEST CONTINENT. It is the western part of the great Eurasian landmass. The Ural Mountains in Russia are the dividing line between Europe and Asia, so only about one-third of Russia is in Europe. It is the only inhabited continent totally outside the tropics.

A continent of peninsulas

In many places the surrounding seas have invaded the land, making Europe a continent of peninsulas – projections of land into the sea. In the north, Scandinavia is a peninsula, in the west, Spain, and in the south, Italy and Greece. Even the islands of Great Britain are a peninsula. They were once joined to France. The two countries are only temporarily separated by the English Channel, and one day they will rejoin.

Europe's climate

Even the center of the continent is quite close to the sea, which influences the climate, giving Europe mild weather. Only northern Scandinavia and Russia are close to the Arctic Circle. There, the summers are cool and at midsummer, the sun shines at midnight. During the icy winters, the sky glows with the northern lights.

▲ In Europe's mild climate, the sun-loving grape vine grows as far north as the German Rhine River

ICELAND

Arctic Circle

ISLAND OF SURTSEY p44–45

Atlantic Ocean

Mt. Galdhopiggen ▲

NORWAY

SCANDIN

GIANT'S CAUSEWAY p48–49

North Sea

IRELAND

GREAT BRITAIN

ENGLISH CHANNEL

GERMANY

E U R O

FRANCE

The Alps

▲ SWITZERLAND

Mont Blanc

PORTUGAL

SPAIN

○ Cabo da Roca

Mediterranean Sea

ITALY

Sicily

North Cape

Ural Mountains

ASIA

RUSSIA

GREECE

METEORA *p46–47*

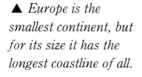
Matapan

▲ *The Alps are Europe's youngest mountains and they have the highest peaks.*

FACTS ABOUT EUROPE

♦ Europe's total area is about 3,800,000 square miles (9,842,000 square kilometers).

♦ From North Cape in Norway (71°12'), the mainland's northernmost point, to Cape Matapan in Greece (36°29'N), the southernmost point, is 2,400 miles (3,862 kilometers).

♦ From Cabo da Roca in Portugal (8°30'W), the most westerly point, to the Ural Mountains in Russia (60°E), which form the eastern boundary, is 3,000 miles (4,800 kilometers).

♦ Mont Blanc, on the French and Italian border in the Alps, is Europe's highest mountain. It is 15,771 feet (4,807 meters) above sea level.

▲ *Europe is the smallest continent, but for its size it has the longest coastline of all.*

▶ *Great forests like this English oak forest once covered much of Europe. Most have been cut down to make room for towns and farmland.*

ISLAND OF SURTSEY

THE TINY ISLAND of Surtsey is one of the newest parts of the world. On November 15, 1963, it appeared in the Atlantic Ocean to the south of Iceland. It is the summit of a volcano that erupted from the sea floor, and rose 425 feet (130 meters) to the surface.

Surtsey is part of the Westman Islands group, which lies to the south of Iceland. Its birth was not a surprise, because geologists know that a volcano might erupt around Iceland at any time. This is because Iceland lies at the northern end of the mid-Atlantic Ridge. A few of the summits of this long undersea mountain range just reach the surface.

The mid-Atlantic Ridge marks the junction of three continental plates: the American and the Eurasian plates in the north, and the African plate further south. Along the Ridge, the plates are moving away from one another. As they pull apart, volcanoes form, bringing lava from the depths of the Earth up to the sea floor.

The material first erupted by the Surtsey volcano was ash and a light material called tephra. Normally, this would be washed away by the sea before an island could form, but later, lava erupted. In time, this hardened to form rock strong enough to resist erosion by the sea.

By 1965, activity from the volcano cone had almost ceased. By then, Surtsey had grown to more than 1 square mile (2.5 square kilometers).

▶ *Surtsey began as a smoke column 50,000 feet (15,000 meters) high, and about 400,000 tons a day of ash and exploding volcanic bombs.*

▼ *Waves washing into the volcano cone caused massive steam explosions.*

WILDLIFE ON SURTSEY

A tiny midge, *Diamesa zernii,* was the first life seen on Surtsey on May 14, 1964. A moth, *Plutella agrotis*, was spotted in August. Next, two weevils of the *Otiorhynchus* species landed aboard some driftwood. Sea rocket seeds blew in on the wind in 1966, but their shoots were killed by an ash fall. The first plant to survive was *Funeria*, a moss which grows on burned ground. By 1967 moss had turned a hillside brown. Guillemots were the first birds to nest on the island.

Guillemot

Midge

Weevil

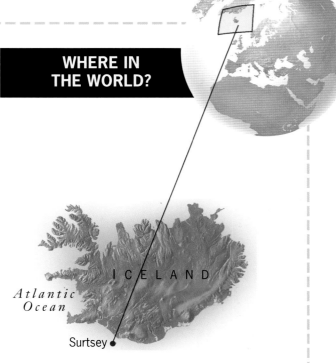

I CELAND

Atlantic Ocean

Surtsey

♦ Surtsey is the most southerly island in the Westman group of islands which lie off the southern coast of Iceland.

SURTSEY DIARY

1963

November 14, 07.15 hours A cook aboard a fishing vessel reported a ship on fire.
10.15 hours Smoke column 12,000 feet (3,600 meters) high seen rising from the sea.
November 15 The first land appeared above the surface of the sea.
By late November The volcano had started to erupt lava.
By December 30 A volcanic cone had formed 500 feet (150 meters) high and half a mile (800 meters) in diameter. The volcano erupted about 180,000 tons of lava an hour. It added about 4,800 square yards (4,000 square meters) a day to the island. Lava raced downhill from the crater rim at about 25 miles (40 kilometers) an hour.

1964-1965

Eruptions from the cone continued, but slowed. During 1965 they almost ceased.

After 1965

Winter storms altered Surtsey from an almost round island into a pear-shaped one by eroding some areas and depositing material in others.

HOW SURTSEY WAS FORMED

Lava erupted by volcanoes is creating new land along the mid-Atlantic Ridge. The continental plates are splitting apart along this mountain chain beneath the ocean. As a result, the Atlantic Ocean is widening by about 2 1/2 inches (1 centimeter) a year.

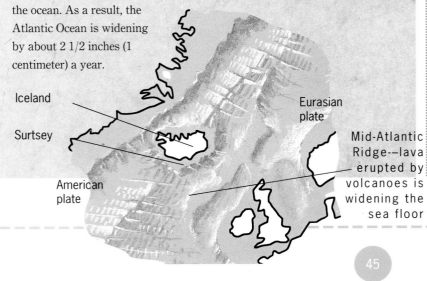

Iceland

Surtsey

American plate

Eurasian plate

Mid-Atlantic Ridge-–lava erupted by volcanoes is widening the sea floor

METEORA

T HE NAME "Meteora" is Greek for "high in the air." This is the perfect name for a natural wonder on the western edge of the Plain of Thessaly in mainland Greece. At the foot of the Pindus Mountains, more than 60 huge stone pillars stand as though guarding the plains below. They average 1,000 feet (300 meters) high, but a few are nearly twice this height.

The pillars are made of sandstone and conglomerate. Conglomerate is a hard, pebbly sedimentary rock. It is formed from the pebbles and gravel carried down a mountain by a fast-flowing river, and dropped on lower land. A river deposits many layers of stones. Over millions of years, they are compressed (squeezed together), until they become rock.

The Meteora rocks are all that remains of a large upland area called a "massif" that once covered the surrounding countryside. The massif was broken into big blocks by deep cracks. Water from the nearby River Pinios and its tributaries ran into the cracks. Sand and pebbles carried by the water carved the cracks wider and deeper, until they became ravines.

Eventually, the rivers wore most of the massif away, leaving huge stumps of rock. These are the only evidence remaining to tell us of a lost land surface.

Meteora's dramatic towers make a spectacular sight, rising from the plain. Clinging to the tops of many of the crags are monasteries that were built in medieval times.

WILDLIFE OF METEORA

Egyptian vulture

Grecian fir

The Egyptian vulture builds its nest of sticks lined with dung and hair on ledges on the Meteora rocks. It hunts on plains and feeds on dead animals and on food and rubbish left by people. The Grecian fir grows on the crags of Meteora.

◀ *Meteora's rocks are a spectacular sight at the foot of the Pindus Mountains in Greece.*

▼ *At the top of 24 of the rock towers are monasteries. They were built about 500 years ago by monks seeking a refuge from the world. Most are now deserted.*

WHERE IN THE WORLD?

Meteora ▲ Mt. Olympus
Kalambaka ● River Pinios
Plain of Thessaly
Pindus Mountains
Aegean Sea
GREECE

♦ Meteora is in central Greece, where the River Pinios emerges from deep canyons in the Pindus Mountains and flows into the Plain of Thessaly.

♦ The plain is about 500 feet (150 meters) above sea level. The Pindus Mountains rise to about 10,000 feet (3,000 meters).

♦ Hermits lived on the pinnacles and in the caves of Meteora in the 800s, and the first monasteries were founded in the 1000s. The monks climbed up the rocks using ladders which they pulled up behind them. Food was hoisted up in baskets.

♦ The bronze Aesculapian snake, *Elaphe longissima*, was sacred to the Ancient Greeks because they believed it had healing powers. Its image is used today by physicians as a symbol of healing. It survives in isolated, rocky habitats, such as Meteora. It grows up to 6 feet (1.8 meters) long, and is a good climber – but it is not dangerous. It eats lizards, and is not a poisonous snake.

THE GIANT'S CAUSEWAY

THE GIANT'S CAUSEWAY got its name because it looks like a great path of stepping stones going out into the sea. (A causeway is a raised path built across shallow water). Local legends say that it was built by an Irish giant called Finn McCool so that he could step acrss the sea to Scotland. The Giant's Causeway is on the coast of County Antrim in Northern Ireland. There are similar rocks on the Scottish islands of Staffa and Mull, and in some other parts of the world, such as Yellowstone National Park in the U.S.

The Giant's Causeway is an astonishing cluster of thousands of stone columns. Behind the Causeway are strangely shaped cliffs, also made of stone columns. The columns are polygonal (many sided), so it is hard to believe that they originated millions of years ago as a pool of lava 350 feet (106 meters) deep. The volcanic activity that built it once affected northwest Britain, Iceland, and Greenland, as well as Northern Ireland.

THE STORY IN THE STONES

Sixty million years ago, shortly after the dinosaurs became extinct, huge volcanoes erupted in the area. In time, much of their lavas eroded away. Later, at the time the Alps were being built in southern Europe, great pressures occurred in the Earth's crust. These pressures may have caused big cracks to open in the ground. Another kind of lava, called basalt, flowed from them. Basalt is a lava that contains very little gas, so it does not erupt explosively, but flows over the countryside. Huge basalt flows covered much of northwest Britain. In County Antrim, some of it ran into a deep hole, part of a former river valley, where it cooled and hardened very slowly. Because the process was so slow, as it cooled, the basalt cracked into thousands of columns. Their tops have now been worn away, leaving the columns you can see today on the Giant's Causeway.

North Channel

Giant's Causeway

Antrim Plateau

Antrim Mts.

County Antrim

◄ *The strangely shaped cliffs and rocks along Ireland's Antrim coast are the remains of lava flows that occurred millions of years ago.*

▲ *There are about 37,000 columns in the Giant's Causeway. Most are six-sided, but some have four, five, seven, and even eight sides.*

♦ The Giant's Causeway is on the Antrim Plateau on the north coast of County Antrim in Northern Ireland.

♦ Not all the columns stand upright. "The Giant's Gate" is the name of a row of tilted columns, and some columns lie horizontal.

♦ Lumps of hard basalt found in layers of coloured rocks were called "Giant's Eyes" by local people.

♦ Fossils show that part of The Giant's Causeway was once covered by soil in which tropical plants once grew.

♦ Light patches in the Causeway cliffs are the remains of huge bubbles of superheated steam and gases in the boiling lava from which they formed.

WILDLIFE OF IRELAND'S NORTHERN COAST

Seabirds that live along the Causeway coast include fulmar petrels, Manx shearwaters, eider ducks, and cormorants, as well as the more widespread oystercatchers, gannets, gulls, guillemots, razorbills, and shags.

Oystercatcher

Fulmar

ASIA

ASIA IS THE LARGEST continent, the eastern part of the Eurasian landmass. Most of the countries of the Middle East, and the countries of the Far East, are in Asia. Millions of years ago, the northeast tip of Asia was joined to North America. Now, the Bering Strait, a shallow sea about 50 miles (80 kilometres) wide, separates the two. In the south, Asia and Africa are joined at the Isthmus of Suez, but geologists think the African plate will eventually split away.

Asia spans both northern and southern hemispheres. North Asia lies within the Arctic Circle. Parts of the northern coast are icebound for much of the year. Yet the equator passes through the archipelago (island group) of Malaysia and Indonesia, so southern Asia's climate is warm.

Colliding continents

This continent is so huge it is carried on three plates. Most of Asia lies on the vast Eurasian plate. Geologists call India a subcontinent because it is carried on its own plate. About 100 million years ago, these two plates started to collide. This collision has thrown up the Himalayas and other high southern mountains.

Turkey floats on one small plate. It is one of the most geologically active places in the world. Japan and the other islands on Asia's southern and eastern edges are part of a ring of active volcanoes and other geological activity around the edges of the Pacific Ocean. This "ring of fire" marks the meeting of the Eurasian and the Pacific plates.

Asia's variety

But only people living on the continent's southern and eastern edges are affected by volcanoes and earthquakes. Most of Asia's vast interior is stable. Its landscapes range from the lake-dotted tundra of Russia's far north and the vast, grassy plains, called steppes, of central Russia, to the dense rainforests of South East Asia. In the far west are the searing hot deserts of Arabia, and in the east is Mongolia's huge, cold Gobi Desert. Asia contains some of the world's most spectacular scenery.

Arctic Circle

EUROPE

R

PAMUKKALE *p52–53*

TURKEY   Caucasus Mountains   Caspian Sea

CAPPADOCIA *p54–55*

Isthmus of Suez

DEAD SEA *p60–61*

MIDDLE EAST

▼ *The Dead Sea is a long, narrow saltwater lake between Israel and Jordan in the Middle East. It is surrounded by hot, sandy deserts.*

◄ *In parts of Turkey, ancient lava flows have been worn into strange rock formations.*

FACTS ABOUT ASIA

♦ Asia covers 17 million square miles (44 million square kilometers) – 30 percent of the Earth's land area.

♦ Asia's western border is an imaginary line along the eastern side of the Ural Mountains, bending southwest along the northern shore of the Caspian Sea to the Caucasus Mountains, and around the coast of Turkey. Its easternmost point is East Cape, 170'W. These longitudes are 6,000 miles (9,600 kilometers) apart.

♦ Asia's most northerly point is Cape Chelyuskin in Russia, 78°30' N. The southernmost point is Singapore in Malaysia, 76 miles (122 kilometers) north of the equator. The two are 8,609 kilometers (5,350 miles) apart.

Bering Strait

Cape Chelyuskin

ASIA

MONGOLIA

Gobi Desert

FAR EAST

JAPAN
Mt. Fuji ▲
Honshu

MT. EVERSEST *p62–63*

Himalayas

CHINA

GUILIN *p58–59*

SOUTH EAST ASIA

MALAYSIA

Equator

Singapore

INDONESIA

▲ *Mount Fuji on the island of Honshu is Japan's highest mountain. It is one of a ring of active volcanoes encircling the Pacific.*

▼ *Bamboo forests cover parts of tropical South China.*

PAMUKKALE

PAMUKKALE, IN WESTERN TURKEY, is an amazing river of hot water, which leaves a trail of white rock wherever it flows.

The river begins as a spring that emerges from inside a hill. Dissolved in the river water are minerals from underground, such as calcium carbonate. This is the main mineral in chalk and limestone. As the water flows downhill, it cools and can no longer hold so much calcium carbonate. All along the river's course, this mineral is deposited as a white rock rather like marble, called travertine.

This way of forming rock is called "mineralization." It usually takes thousands of years, but in Pamukkale it happens so fast you can watch it. A stick or a straw hat put into the water is soon white with travertine, and in a few days it is covered with rock and looks like a fossil.

Travertine soon builds up and fills the channel where the river flows. When its bed becomes blocked, the river finds new routes to flow along. Each new route is quickly marked by a glistening white travertine trail. The trail flows downhill in a series of petrified waterfalls ("petrified" means "turned to stone"). Water has dripped over the edges of stone terraces, creating strangely shaped stalactites and coating the rocks so that they look like piles of cotton.

Geologically, Turkey is very active. The huge Eurasian plate is squeezing it from the north, and the Arabian plate is squeezing it from the south. The friction between these plates and the single plate that carries Turkey generates heat. It is this volcanic heat that warms the river at Pamukkale.

▲ *From a distance, the terraces in the hillside at Pamukkale look as if they have been wrapped in shining white cotton. They have given this extraordinary place its name. "Pamukkale" is a Turkish word meaning "cotton castle."*

THE THREAT FROM TOURISM

People have bathed in Pamukkale's river for more than 2,000 years. They have always believed its waters have health-giving properties. In the 200s B.C., the Romans founded a town, Hierapolis, for people who wanted to drink or bathe in the hot spring water. But today, Pamukkale has so many tourists that the travertine terraces are in danger of being damaged.

Modern visitors have to bathe in specially built pools. Many governments impose strict rules in national parks and wild places to prevent visitors from harming the natural wonders they come to admire.

▲ *An "iron waterfall" has colored this rock brown and red. The river waters contain iron and many other minerals, as well as dissolved limestone rock.*

▶ *Water dripping down the terraces at Pamukkale hardens into bizarre stalactites within a few days. Stalactites can take hundreds of years to form from droplets of water.*

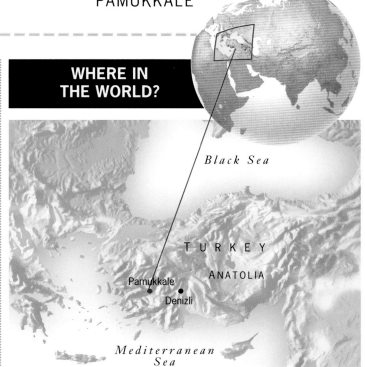

Black Sea

TURKEY

ANATOLIA

Pamukkale
Denizli

Mediterranean
Sea

♦ Pamukkale is in western Anatolia in Turkey, 12 miles (19 kilometers) north of the provincial capital of Denizli.

♦ It is 1,150 feet (350 meters) above sea level. The Cotton Castle terraces form a cliff 400 feet (122 meters) high.

♦ On the plateau above the terraces are the ruined Roman town of Hierapolis. Here, special pools have been built where visitors can bathe in the warm spring waters.

♦ The travertine deposits have covered the valley floor 6 feet 6 inches (2 meters) deep.

♦ The waters emerge from the hot spring at a temperature of about 97°F (36°C). They contain iron, sodium chloride (salt), sulphuric acid, and magnesium, as well as calcium carbonate (limestone).

♦ The Eurasian plate and the Arabian plate are acting like scissor blades, squeezing the small Turkish plate between them. If you try to catch a small, hard object between the blades of a pair of scissors, the object shoots out from between them very quickly. This is why the westward movement of the small Turkish plate is much faster than the Arabian plate's movement north, or the huge Eurasian plate's southward movement.

CAPPADOCIA

IN CENTRAL TURKEY there is a region so fantastic that when people in Europe first heard of it they refused to believe it existed. Cappadocia looks more like a moonscape than an Earth landscape. It is covered with a crust of oddly shaped rocks colored white, yellowy brown, pink, and mauve. Down the slopes of some of the hills cascade smooth white stone terraces that look like billowing sand dunes – until you touch them. And in some of the valleys the rocks have formed columns that look like spindly towers and spires.

To the east of Cappadocia is an extinct volcano called Erciyas Dagi. When it last erupted, about 10 million years ago, it covered an immense area, first with ash and then with lava. Over the centuries, these were worked on by the forces of rain and frost.

At first, deep canyons were worn in the volcanic plain. Then these widened and the rock was cut into small sections by side canyons. Today, only pinnacles and spires of soft tufa remain, protected by caps of hard basalt rock.

Hundreds of years ago, people dug into the soft tufa cones. They made some into houses, with doors and windows, and lived in them. In the 1700s, the first European explorer to see Cappadocia thought that its fairytale landscape had been made by people, not by nature.

A FAIRYTALE LANDSCAPE SCULPTED BY THE WEATHER

For millions of years the small plate that carries Turkey has moved west by about 4 1/2 inches (115 millimeters) a year. Earthquakes occur along one of the boundaries between the Turkish plate and the Arabian plate to the south of it. This boundary is called the Anatolian Fault. More than 10 million years ago, three volcanoes erupted in central Anatolia. Erciyas Dagi was the largest. It erupted for thousands of years, covering an immense area with ash and deep rivers of lava. The ash became compressed into tufa, a soft rock. The lava hardened into basalt rock. As the lava cooled, it cracked. Over centuries, the cracks were widened and deepened by wind, rain, frost, and sun. In time, the lava became criss-crossed with deep canyons. The weather eroded the tufa into columns and pinnacles separated by ravines. The hard basalt formed a cap, protecting the tufa from eroding away.

WHERE IN THE WORLD?

Black Sea

TURKEY

● Kayseri

Cappadocia

ANATOLIA

Taurus Mts.

Mediterranean Sea

♦ Cappadocia is in the Anatolian Highlands in east central Turkey, 200 miles (322 kilometers) southeast of Ankara. These hills average 6,000 feet (1,800 meters) in height.

♦ The region covers an area of 50 square miles (130 square kilometers).

♦ Erciyas Dagi is Turkey's highest mountain. It is 12,850 feet (3,917 meters) high.

♦ The volcanic ash is so soft that the Early Christians carved churches and monasteries into it. The pinnacles once housed more than 30,000 people.

▲ *These columns of soft tufa are called "fairy chimneys." Their caps of hard basalt rock look rather like chimney pots.*

▶ *Cappadocia's first European visitor was a Frenchman living in the 1700s called Paul Lucas. He wrote that he had found an amazing city of cone-shaped houses.*

LAKE BAIKAL

IN WILD SOUTHERN SIBERIA, close to Russia's border with Mongolia, is a huge and mysterious lake. Lake Baikal is Asia's largest freshwater lake. It covers an area of 12,162 square miles (31,500 square kilometers). It is fed by the waters of more than 300 rivers. But only one river, the Lower Angara, carries its waters away.

Baikal is the deepest lake in the world. Surveyors have worked out that in some places its bed is almost 1 mile (1.6 kilometers) from its surface. Sometimes, major storms disturb its surface, but they cannot reach its great, silent depths. The surface is kept warm by currents of incoming river water. But the depths are as black as night, icy cold, and lifeless.

Lake Baikal is as old as its surrounding mountain ranges. One reason why geologists know this is because more than 80 percent of its wildlife species can be found nowhere else. More than 1,000 species of animals, and over 800 plant species live in and around it. They have changed since the lake was formed, and since that time few new species have settled there. Today, pollution caused by industries located beside the lake is killing the fishes and other wildlife that lives in and around it at a frightening rate.

But Lake Baikal may mark the beginning of new changes in the land. Earthquakes often occur in the region, and some alter the shape of the lake's edge. Some geologists think that the lake could be the starting point for the creation of a new sea, which will eventually split Asia in two.

▶ *Lake Baikal's rocky shoreline. It lies in a region of taiga, or coniferous forest. Siberian stone pine is the dominant tree.*

◀ *The surface water of Lake Baikal is frozen throughout the winter, from September until May.*

HOW LAKE BAIKAL WAS FORMED

Lake Baikal is long, narrow, and deep. It was formed 20 million years ago, when the mountains of central Asia were pushed up. The forces caused faults and cracks to develop in the rocks, and a huge trench to open. This slowly widened into a long, narrow basin. This basin filled with water and so became Lake Baikal.

R U S S I A

Siberian Plain
Lake Baikal
Irkutsk □

■Ulan Bator
M O N G O L I A

♦ Lake Baikal is in southern Siberia in the state of Russia in central Asia. It lies just north of the state of Mongolia.

♦ It is 395 miles (636 kilometers) long and averages 30 miles (48.3 kilometers) wide.

♦ Its maximum depth is 5,710 feet (1,740 meters). It has a total volume of 5,500 cubic miles (22,924 cubic kilometers). This is said to be as much water as is in all five of the Great Lakes of North America.

♦ The Baikal State Nature Reserve was set up in 1979. It covers an area of 640 square miles (1,657 square kilometers).

♦ Lake Baikal is in an area that is hot in summer but intensely cold in winter, but the lake is so large that it affects the local climate, making the winters slightly warmer and the summers slightly cooler.

♦ Hot mineral springs near to Lake Baikal are an indication of recent volcanic activity.

♦ About 800 species of flowering plants, 37 mammal species, and 260 species of birds live in the taiga surrounding the lake.

WILDLIFE OF LAKE BAIKAL

Longwing sculpin

A total 400 plant species and 960 animal species are found only in the Baikal State Nature Reserve. The Baikal seal is the world's only freshwater seal. It is thought to be descended from Arctic seals that migrated inland, perhaps by river, millions of years ago. The longwing sculpin is one of several fish unique to its waters. But pollution from industries around the lake is damaging the environment.

Baikal seal

GUILIN

WESTERNERS have always been amazed to see mountains looking like salt cellars in Chinese paintings. They thought they must be imaginary mountains dreamed up by the artists. But this picturesque scenery is real. It exists in Guilin in southeast China.

Guilin is one of the most beautiful parts of China. It has been a tourist spot for more than 1,000 years. Flowing through the area is the wide, peaceful Gui Jiang – the Gui River. Its flat plain is almost the only flat land in the upland region of southern China.

Rising out of the plain on either side of the river are hundreds of strangely shaped mountains. Many have steep, almost straight sides and dome-shaped tops. One on the Gui River plain is called Elephant Trunk Hill because it looks like an elephant dipping its trunk into the river to drink.

Guilin's hills are made of limestone that has worn down over time into unusual shapes. Geologists call landscapes of eroded limestone "karst" scenery. It exists in other places – in former Yugoslavia and Ireland. But nowhere is it so amazing as in the hills of Guilin.

WILDLIFE OF GUILIN

Great cormorant

"Guilin" means "Cassia Forest" in Chinese. The bark, fruit, and oil of the cassia tree have been used for centuries as a spice, a flavoring, and a medicine. Bamboo is also native to the region. Chinese artists of the 1600s painted the mountains of Guilin with fir trees growing at angles from their sides and summits. The paintings were true to life – the beautiful Cathay silver fir grows on the Guilin hillsides. Rhesus macaque is one of several monkey species living in the woods. Fishing cormorants are native to waterways in South and Southeast Asia.

Rhesus macaque

▲ Deep inside many of the mountains are long tunnels and huge caves. The Reed Flute Cave is the most famous of several caverns decorated by nature with colorful stalactites and stalagmites, and brilliantly sparkling roofs and walls.

Cathay silver fir

THE STORY OF GUILIN

About 300 million years ago limestone was formed on the bed of a sea that covered much of Southeast Asia. Long afterward, earth movements pushed the limestone up so high above the sea that rocks that were once the sea bed became mountain tops. Wind, rain, and ice wore down their peaks into round hills. Gradually, rainwater which was slightly acid dissolved away channels in the limestone. These channels widened into tunnels and great caverns. In time, the roofs of these caves collapsed, leaving only the hardest rocks standing as isolated hills.

Acid rain dissolves away limestone, forming caves

Porous limestone

Cave roofs fall in

Non-porous rock

Remaining rock strata weather into rounded hills

▲ *The great cormorant swims low on the water surface and dives for its prey. It is called the "fishing cormorant" in South China. Along the Gui River, fishermen use it to catch fish.*

▼ *The Guilin hills are made of ancient limestone that has eroded into domes. These hills rise from about 300 feet (91 meters) to about 800 feet (244 meters) above the plain.*

WHERE IN THE WORLD?

CHINA

Guilin

Guangxi Zhuang

Southern Uplands

Nanning

Hainani I.

♦ Guilin is in the Southern Uplands, a hilly region of southeast China. It is in the Guangxi-Zhuang Autonomous Region, bordering Vietnam.

♦ As well as an area of karst scenery, Guilin is a city on the Gui River plain, among the limestone hills. It was founded about 2,300 years ago. It is now an administrative center.

▼ *Guilin's rounded hills rising from rice paddy fields beside the Gui River, and the caves and tunnels inside them, have been popular with tourists for hundreds of years.*

THE DEAD SEA

EVERYWHERE ON Earth that is more than 300 feet (91 meters) below the level of the oceans is underwater – except for the Dead Sea. The surface of this sea and its surrounding shores are, at their lowest point, 1,286 feet (392 meters) below sea level. So the Dead Sea is the lowest lake on Earth.

It is also the world's saltiest body of natural water. About 55 inches (140 centimeters) of water evaporate from the Dead Sea every year. What remains after the water has evaporated are all the salts and mud that were carried in the waters of the streams and rivers that feed the Dead Sea. They give its water a salt content (called "salinity") as high as 25 per cent. This is extremely salty. By comparison, most seawater has a salinity of 5 per cent.

The Dead Sea is a sparkling blue. But bands of salt line the shores and little saltfloes float on the surface. The water is poisonous to most aquatic life. Only a few bacteria can live in the Dead Sea, so it is well named. But no living thing can sink in it, either. You do not need to know how to swim to bathe in the Dead Sea. The water's density will hold you up.

WILDLIFE AROUND THE DEAD SEA

Nothing lives in the Dead Sea. But on its shores nature reserves have been set up to protect and breed desert wildlife, which has been seriously harmed in recent wars. War drove leopards from the Negev Desert, but they are returning. Gazelles, caracals (a cat species), and foxes inhabit the hills and deserts surrounding the Dead Sea. The fat sand rat is one of many small rodents that live in the desert sands. It often comes out of its burrow in daytime to feed on succulent plants, many of which contain plenty of salt.

Fat sand rat

Leopard

▲ *The Dead Sea lies between two ranges of hills – the Mountains of Moab in Jordan to the east and the Judean Hills in Israel to the west.*

◀ *About 25 percent of the weight of the Dead Sea's water is salt in solution. Bands of salt line its shores, and lumps of gypsum, a white mineral left by evaporating water, are scattered on the seabed.*

A SHRINKING SEA

...ither side of the Dead Sea, mountains rise higher than 3,000 feet (900 meters). Rivers ...ain from their slopes into its waters, and every day the Jordan River deposits ...illions of tons of water into it. But not a stream runs out of it. The water evaporates ...o rapidly that salts dissolved in it ...ystallize into lumps on its ...rface, and the Sea is shrinking. ...he Dead Sea is part of the Great ...ift Valley, a huge system of faults ... the Earth's crust, which runs ...om Syria, through the Red Sea, ...ross East Africa to Mozambique. ...ovements in this fault are also ...aking the Dead Sea smaller.

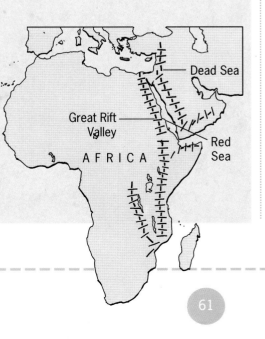

♦ The Dead Sea is in the long Jordan Valley on the Jordan/Israel border.

♦ It is about 34 miles (55 kilometers) long, and averages about 9 miles (14.75 kilometers) wide. Its maximum depth is 1,300 feet (396 meters).

♦ About 19 billion cubic feet (538 million cubic meters) of water flow into it every year, mainly from the River Jordan.

♦ The high rate of evaporation in the hot summer causes the height of the water to vary according to the season of the year. This variation is called a "yearly tide," but it is not like an ocean tide.

MOUNT EVEREST

THE PEAK OF Mount Everest is the Earth's highest point. It is always said to be 29,028 feet (8,848 meters) above sea level, but many surveyors (people who measure land) think it is 29,140 feet (8,882 meters) high.

Mount Everest was measured by British surveyors in 1852. They named it after a famous English surveyor called Sir George Everest, who lived in India in the 1830s.

Mount Everest is in the Himalayas, a huge mountain range which extends into six Asian countries. It is the world's third longest mountain range – 2,983 miles (4,800 kilometers) long. It contains 18 peaks higher than 26,248 feet (8,000 meters), so all of the highest mountains in the world are in the Himalayas.

In the 1800s, geographers studied rocks from the mountains to try to find out why the Himalayas are so high. They found that the range is about 50 million years old – about the same age as the Alps and other high mountains of the world.

The Himalayas balance on the edges of the Indian and the Eurasian plates. The two plates are crashing into each other, and the force of this collision is pushing the land higher than anywhere else on the Earth's surface.

▶ *In the eastern Himalayas, 31 peaks are higher than 25,000 feet (7,600 meters). This mountain range is rising 1 inch (2.5 centimeters) higher every year.*

▶ *Mount Everest stretches across the border between Nepal and China. The Tibetans call this mighty mountain Chomo-lungma, meaning "The Mother Goddess of the Land."*

CHINA

TIBET

Himalayas

Mt. Everest

Sagarmatha
National Park

Katmandu

NEPAL   BHUTAN

INDIA

*Indian
Ocean*

♦ Mount Everest lies toward the eastern end of the Himalaya mountain range, and overlooks one of the high basins of Tibet.

♦ On May 29, 1953, Edmund Hillary, a mountaineer from New Zealand, and a Sherpa (a Tibetan), Tenzing Norkay, were the first climbers to reach the summit of Mount Everest.

♦ Sherpa people told Westerners about a mountain creature they call the "Yeti," or "Abominable Snowman," which lives in the region. Expeditions have looked for it, but although footprints have been found, no expedition has reported seeing one.

THE GREAT CRASH

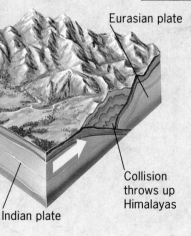

Eurasian plate

Collision
throws up
Himalayas

Indian plate

About 50 million years ago, the plate that carries the Indian subcontinent crashed into the Eurasian continental plate. The huge force of the collision pushed land that was once a seabed 5 miles (8 kilometers) up, to form the lofty Himalaya mountain range. Rocks from the peaks of the Himalayas contain fossils of animals that once lived in the depths of ancient oceans.

SAGARMATHA NATIONAL PARK

Mount Everest is in the Sagarmatha National Park, an area of glaciers, valleys, and lakes, all above 9,842 feet (3,000 meters). Pine and fir trees, and rhododendron shrubs, grow at this height. Animal residents include wolves, black bears, musk deer, and mountain sheep. Native birds include Himalayan griffons and brilliantly coloured pheasants. Jumping spiders live on the slopes of Everest. Some migratory birds fly higher, but this is the highest known animal habitat.

Monal
pheasant

Mountain
sheep

AFRICA

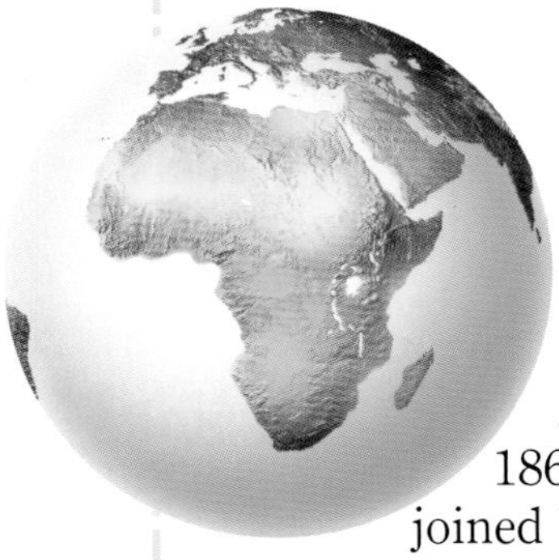

AFRICA IS the second largest continent, after Asia. Until 1869, the two continents were joined between the Red Sea and the Mediterranean Sea, but they were separated by the Suez Canal.

Africa is the largest fragment of Gondwana, the supercontinent that began to break up about 180 million years ago. The Great Rift Valley, which runs therough East Africa from the Red Sea to Zimbabwe and Mozambique, is a sign that Africa is continuing to break up. Geologists believe the African and Eurasian plates will eventually split apart along the Great Rift Valley.

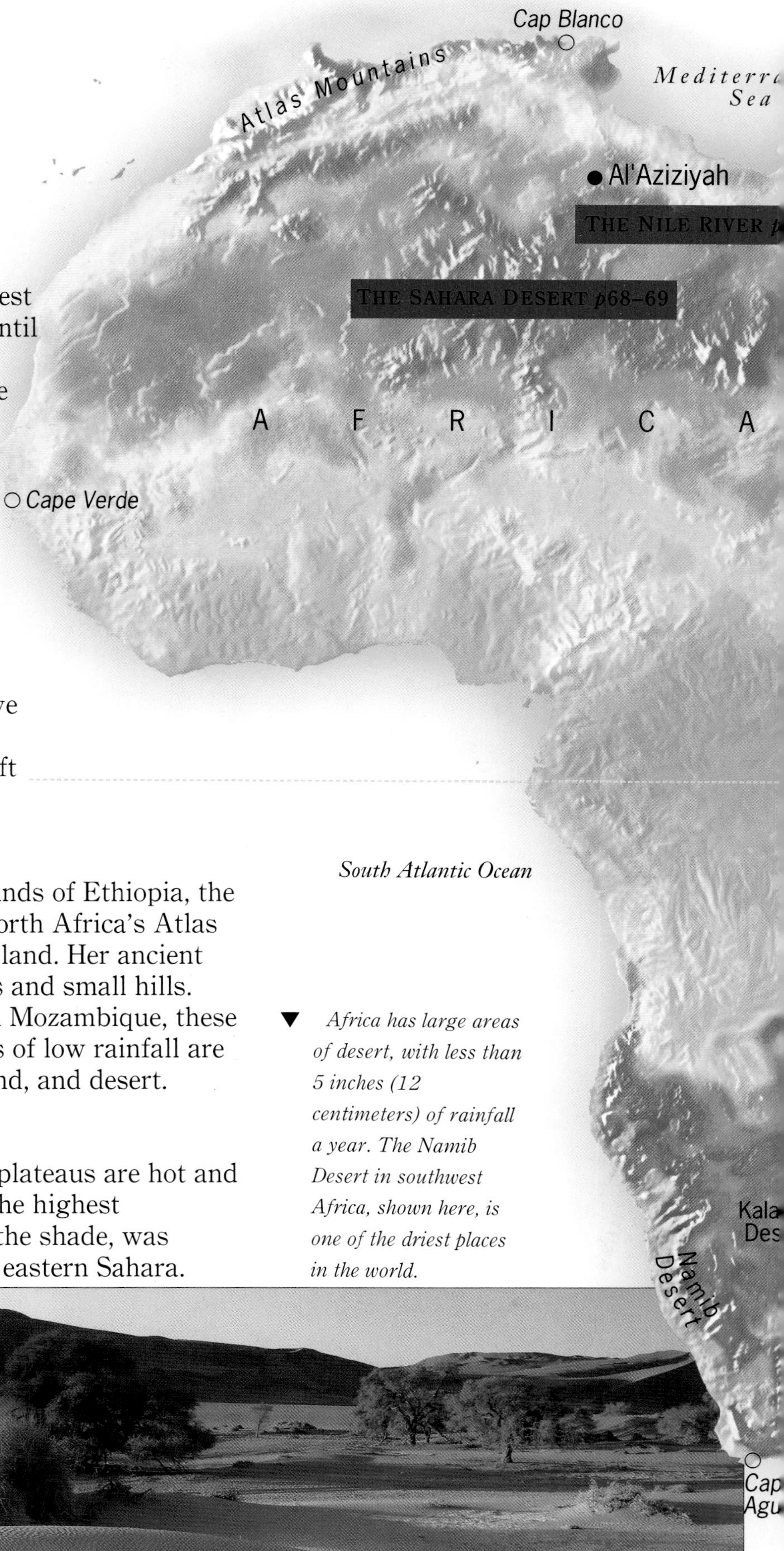

Highlands and lowlands
The volcanoes of East Africa, the Highlands of Ethiopia, the Ruwenzori Mountains in Uganda, and North Africa's Atlas Mountains, are Africa's only really high land. Her ancient mountains have eroded to flat tablelands and small hills. Where rainfall is high, such as Zaire and Mozambique, these are clothed with tropical forests. Regions of low rainfall are covered with bush (shrublands), grassland, and desert.

The hottest place on Earth
Africa lies across the equator. The high plateaus are hot and dry, the coasts hot and humid. In 1922, the highest temperature ever taken, 136°F (58°C) in the shade, was recorded at Al 'Aziziyah, in Libya in the eastern Sahara.

Cap Blanco

Mediterra Sea

● Al'Aziziyah

THE NILE RIVER

THE SAHARA DESERT *p68–69*

A F R I C A

○ Cape Verde

South Atlantic Ocean

▼ *Africa has large areas of desert, with less than 5 inches (12 centimeters) of rainfall a year. The Namib Desert in southwest Africa, shown here, is one of the driest places in the world.*

Kala Des

Namib Desert

○ Cap Agu

Atlas Mountains

Suez
Canal

Red Sea

van
:e ○
:ser

□ Khartoum

hr
l
:zal

THE
GREAT
RIFT
VALLEY
p70-71

○ Lake Assal

Ethiopian
Highlands

Blue
Nile

e Nile

Ras Xufun

RUWENZORI p72-73

Equator

Lake
Victoria

▲ Kirinyaga
(Mt. Kenya)

▲ Mt. Kilimanjaro

Serengeti
Plain

Indian
Ocean

MADAGASCAR

▲ *The Serengeti Plain in Tanzania is part of the Great Rift Valley, which runs through East Africa.*

FACTS ABOUT AFRICA

♦ Africa is the second largest continent, after Asia. It covers an area of 11,700,000 square miles (3,030,000 square kilometers).

♦ Its most westerly point is Cape Verde in Senegal (17°W). Its most easterly point is Ras Xufun, Somalia (51°27'E). At its widest, it is about 4,600 miles (7,360 kilometers) across.

♦ Cape Blanc in Tunisia (37°N) is its most northerly point; Cape Agulhas in South Africa (35°S) is its most southerly point. The greatest distance from north to south is about 5,000 miles (8,000 kilometers).

♦ Africa's highest peak is Mount Kilimanjaro, an ancient volcano in Tanzania, in the Great Rift Valley. It is 19,340 feet (5,895 meters) high. The continent's lowest point is Lake Assal in Djibouti, which is 509 feet (155 meters) below sea level.

▲ *Southern Africa and the northern coast have a Mediterranean-type climate.*

▶ *The peaks of the Ruwenzori Mountains in central Africa, and of Mounts Kenya and Kilimanjaro in the east, are Africa's only areas of permanent snow.*

THE NILE RIVER

THE NILE is the world's longest river. From its source in the hills of Burundi, to the Mediterranean Sea, the Nile is 4,132 miles (6,650 kilometers) long. That is more than 100 miles (150 kilometers) longer than the mighty Amazon River .

For thousands of years, farmers have grown crops on the fertile strip created by the Nile across the eastern Sahara Desert. Each summer the river rose and flooded its banks. When it subsided, they planted seed in the fertile silt it spread across the desert. But not until 1856 did anyone know exactly where the Nile comes from or why it floods each year.

The Nile has more than one source. Some of its headwaters rise south of the equator in Burundi, and flow into the west side of Lake Victoria. From the north side runs a river called the White Nile. It drops 120 feet (37 meters) over the Murchison Falls, then rushes to the Sudan, where the land flattens and the river is slowed in a great marshy area. Almost half its water evaporates or seeps away, but it flows north for another 500 miles (805 kilometers).

At Khartoum, the White Nile is joined by another long river, the Blue Nile. From here, the river is called "The Nile." Then, 200 miles (322 kilometers) further on, the River Atbara adds its waters to the flow. The Blue Nile and the Atbara carry far more water than the longer Nile. Both rise in the Ethiopian Highlands. In summer, rains from the hills swell their waters. These rains cause the annual flooding of the Nile that has given life to the land for the people of Egypt for more than 3,000 years.

▲ *These feluccas moored at Aswan are traditional Nile boats used for fishing and transport. Silt carried by the river is being trapped by the huge new dam at Aswan, so fewer nutrients are flowing downriver to make the Nile Delta fertile.*

WILDLIFE OF THE NILE

Water birds that live along the Nile include the Egyptian goose, the heron, and the ibis – the Ancient Egyptians worshipped the sacred ibis. They made a kind of paper from papyrus, a sedge which grows at the water's edges. The Nile banks are a hiding place for reptiles, such as crocodiles, snakes, and lizards. In the mud along the banks of the Upper Nile, hippopotamuses wallow.

Sacred ibis

Nile crocodile

◀ *The Nile makes a fertile strip about 20 miles (32 kilometers) wide through the eastern Sahara. The river is home to many kinds of fish. The giant Nile perch can weigh up to 300 pounds (136 kilograms).*

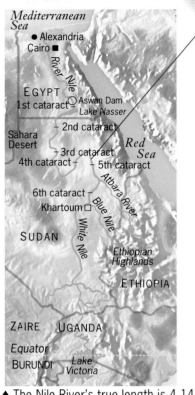

WHERE IN THE WORLD?

♦ The Nile River's true length is 4,145 miles (6,670 kilometers). However, the building of the Aswan Dam and Lake Nasser shortened the river by a few kilometers.

♦ The Nile's drainage basin is estimated to be 1,293,000 square miles (3,349,000 square kilometers). It includes parts of 8 countries, and about 10 percent of Africa's land area.

♦ The Aswan Dam and Lake Nasser, the world's largest artificial lake, were built during the 1960s and opened in 1971. They control the Nile floods and provide electricity.

♦ In six places, the Nile crosses bands of hard rock, causing rapids called "cataracts." In the past, they made navigation difficult.

THE NILE DELTA

A river slows as it approaches the sea. As its speed drops, it drops the sand and mud that it carries. Over thousands of years, layers of silt build up a triangular piece of land called a delta. By about 4000 B.C. the Nile Delta was a mass of lagoons and islands of silt, smoothed by the sea into an arc shape. The river flowed through the delta as a series of streams called "distributaries," which often changed course. Today, much of the Nile Delta is solid land on which towns have been built.

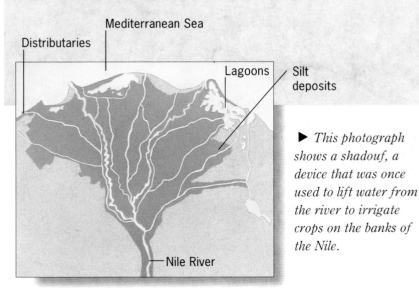

▶ *This photograph shows a shadouf, a device that was once used to lift water from the river to irrigate crops on the banks of the Nile.*

THE SAHARA DESERT

THE VAST SAHARA, largest of the world's deserts, spreads across Africa from the Atlantic Ocean to the Red Sea. The Sahara is a desert because on average fewer than 4 inches (10 centimeters) of rain fall on most of it every year. Murzuq, deep inside Libya, has 0.32 inches (8 millimeters) of rain a year. In some years, no rain falls at all. Sometimes, a whole year's rain falls at once in a single storm, and soaks into the ground.

The low rainfall makes it impossible for most plants to grow. But the desert has a few oases, places where water from underground lakes and rivers wells up through porous layers of rock, and forms a water hole or even a lake. Trees and other plants grow around the water.

In some parts of the desert dew may form at night. Dew forms when water that has evaporated into the air above the desert cools in the cold night air and condenses on the ground. It is a source of liquid for desert plants and animals.

The desert is not all flat. Rocky uplands cover large areas. Some hills are 11,000 feet (3,353 meters) above sea level.

The Sahara is getting bigger. Some areas have dried out because of changes in the pattern of rainfall, but many are barren because of poor care by people.

▶ *Regions of huge sand dunes called "ergs" cover about 100,000 square miles (260,000 square kilometers) of the Sahara. The world's highest sand dune, measured in the Grand Erg Oriental in east central Algeria, was 1,410 feet (430 meters) high and over 3 miles (5 kilometers) long.*

▼ *Only about 15 percent of the Sahara Desert consists of seas of sand dunes. There are large areas of uplands and stony plains.*

MOVING SAND DUNES

Dunes are formed when wind drives sand into mounds. Some dunes have not moved for thousands of years. Others, called barchans, move up to 36 feet (11 meters) a year. Strong winds blow sand high in the air, causing sandstorms. Small grains may be carried far away. Heavier grains are dropped nearby.

❶ Small object causes sand to pile up.

❷ Turbulence causes sand grains on steep face to fall forward.

❸ Sand grains at sides of dune blow forward, forming crescent.

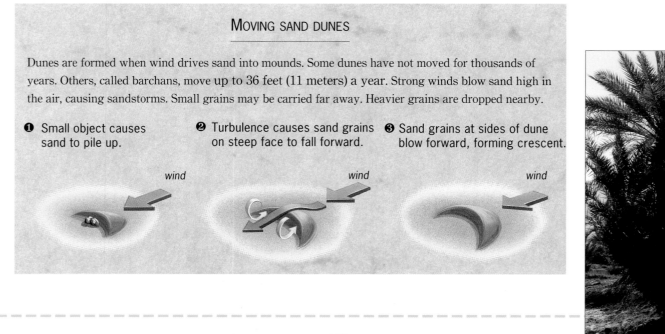

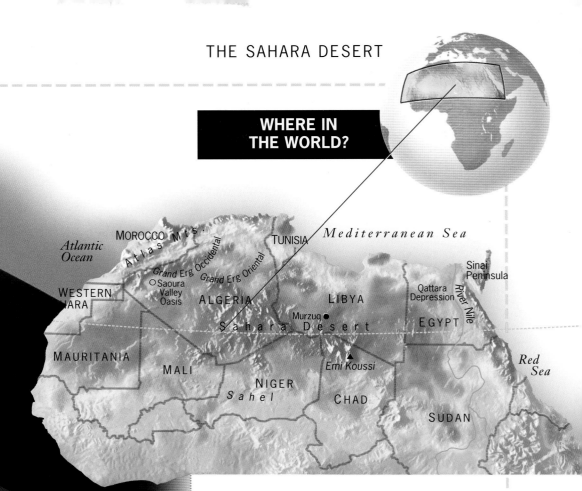

Mediterranean Sea

Atlantic Ocean

MOROCCO *Atlas Mts.* TUNISIA

Sinai Peninsula

Grand Erg Occidental

Grand Erg Oriental

○ Saoura Valley Oasis

WESTERN SAHARA

ALGERIA

LIBYA

Qattara Depression

River Nile

EGYPT

Murzuq ●

S a h a r a   D e s e r t

MAURITANIA

MALI

Emi Koussi ▲

Red Sea

NIGER

Sahel

CHAD

SUDAN

♦ The Sahara Desert covers much of Africa north of about 15°N of the equator, an area of 3,579,000 square miles (9,269,000 square kilometers).

♦ From the Atlas Mountains and the Mediterranean Sea in the north to the dry grasslands of the Sahel in the south is a distance of between 800 and 1,400 miles (1,280 and 2,250 kilometers).

♦ At its widest, the Sahara is 3,200 miles (5,150 kilometers) from east to west.

♦ At its lowest point – the Qattara Depression in Egypt – the Sahara is 36 feet (132 meters) below sea level. The highest peak is Emi Koussi in the Tibesti Massif in Chad. It is 11,204 feet (3,415 meters) above sea level.

♦ Temperatures range from more than 109°F (43°C) in the sun to below freezing at night. The highest recorded daytime temperature was 136.4°F (58°C).

▼ *Date palms and rushes flourish in an oasis in the Saoura River Valley on the edge of the Grand Erg Oriental in Algeria.*

WILDLIFE OF THE DESERT

In daytime the desert is unbearably hot, for there is nothing to deflect or diffuse the sunlight. Many animals lie hidden all day in cool burrows below the sand. At night, the temperature drops, and they come out to feed. The desert jerboa eats seeds, roots, and insects. The fennec fox lives on locusts, lizards, and nestlings. Most of the water they need comes from their food.

Jerboa

Fennec fox

THE GREAT RIFT VALLEY

THERE ARE PLACES in East Africa where you can stand on the edge of a cliff that runs left and right as far as you can see. Before you is a great valley, perhaps 35 miles (56 kilometers) wide. This is part of the Great Rift Valley, a huge gash in the Earth's surface. It runs 4,000 miles (6,437 kilometers) or more, from Syria southeast toward Mozambique.

The Great Rift Valley is not a single, straight cut, but many. One major branch runs along the east side of the Congo River basin. Another runs near Nairobi in Kenya.

Glaciers and rivers did not carve the Great Rift Valley. It was formed by the immense forces that move the continents across the Earth. At its deepest, the tear in the land is about 8,200 feet (2,500 meters) deep. But the valley sides are nowhere as high as this. They are filled with layers of lava up to 1 mile (1.6 kilometers) thick. The lava flowed from many volcanoes along the line of the rift.

The lava erupted by the volcanoes filled the trenches and expanded them, pushing the sides of the valley further apart, so creating new land. This is still happening, but very slowly. In East Africa the valley has widened by about 6 miles (10 kilometers) in about 10 million years. But in the north, it has widened by about 200 miles (320 kilometers) in the same amount of time, to form the Red Sea. Some geologists think the valley will widen even more, until eventually, Africa splits in two.

▼ *In places, the Rift Valley floor has filled with water. The line of the rift is marked by long, narrow lakes. The waters of this salt lake contain soda and many other minerals.*

CREATION OF A CONTINENT

• THIRTY MILLION YEARS AGO Africa and Arabia formed one continent, but movements in the Earth began to force the African and Arabian plates apart, creating the Red Sea.

• FIVE MILLION YEARS AGO Earth movements began to create the Great Rift Valley. Heat from within the Earth made the land bulge out. Later, part of it collapsed, and volcanoes erupted.

Land bulges outward

Magma

• BY 3 MILLION YEARS AGO lava rose between the lowlands and the mountains. It spread across the valley floor, forcing the valley sides apart, and hardened into a basalt plain.

• FROM 2 MILLION YEARS AGO lava rose through new cracks, appearing as a line of volcanoes along Africa's eastern edge.

• Now land to the east of the Great Rift Valley is surrounded by faults.

• IN 30 MILLION YEARS the Somali Plate may be a new continent floating in the Indian Ocean.

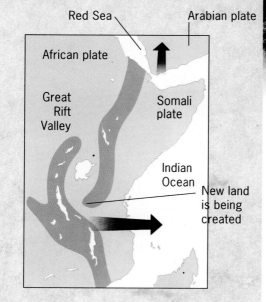

Red Sea

Arabian plate

African plate

Great Rift Valley

Somali plate

Indian Ocean

New land is being created

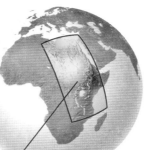

Mediterranean Sea SYRIA
ASIA
EGYPT
Red Sea
SUDAN
ETHIOPIA
Great Rift Valley
Congo River
UGANDA
KENYA
■ Nairobi
RWANDA
BURUNDI
Mt. Kilimanjaro
Lake TANZANIA *Indian Ocean*
Tanganyika
ZIARE
MOZAMBIQUE

♦ The eastern branch of the Great Rift system begins in north Syria. It runs south through the Red Sea and the Dead Sea, then through East Africa. The western branch runs roughly along the Congo River.

♦ Lake Tanganyika, one of the Rift Valley's deepest lakes, is 4,823 feet (1,470 meters) deep.

▲ *Mount Kilimanjaro in Tanzania is an extinct volcano, but there are at least nine active volcanoes in the Great Rift Valley. Earthquakes and hot springs are other signs of continuing volcanic activity in this unstable region.*

Giraffe

WILDLIFE OF THE SERENGETI

The Serengeti Plain in Tanzania is a part of the Great Rift Valley that shelters many large animals, including giraffes, zebra, antelope, such as Thomson's gazelle, other grazing animals, and predators, such as lions. Threatened species, such as the African elephant and the African hunting dog, survive there.

Zebra

African elephant

Thomson's gazelle

Lion

RUWENZORI

I<small>N THE</small> 200<small>S</small>, an ancient Greek mapmaker called Ptolemy drew a map showing where the River Nile began. He had heard a story from a traveling merchant called Diogenes that it was formed from melting snows on a huge range of mountains far to the south of Egypt, with lakes spreading out from their foothills. He called these imaginary hills "The Mountains of the Moon."

In the 1880s, the first European explorers saw these incredible mountains where the mapmaker had predicted. They stand out of the surrounding plain like a great island, their summits silvery with snow, yet they are near the equator. Africans call them "Ruwenzori," meaning "The Rainmaker," because the mountains get about 75 inches (190 centimeters) of rain a year. The rain creates many streams. Some feed the White Nile, but they are not the River Nile's true source. Its headwaters (tributary rivers that form its source) are in Burundi.

The Ruwenzori are snowcapped because they are so high. The highest peak is Mount Margherita, 16,798 feet (5,120 meters) above sea level. Five other peaks are higher than 15,000 feet (4,572 meters). The range is perhaps only 2 million years old, yet the rocks it is made of are much older. They were squeezed up into mountains by the forces that formed the Great Rift Valley in the east.

Almost all year, the Ruwenzori are capped with cloud, which hides their beautiful white peaks. Little wildlife lives on their icy slopes. But the Ruwenzori is like an island in a sea of lowlands. Its climate and environment are very different from those of the surrounding region. The plants and animals that live on the lower slopes of the mountains are among the strangest in the world.

▲ *The Portal Peaks of the Ruwenzori are about 14,400 feet (4,389 meters) high. Here their tops are eerily shrouded in clouds. Tribal people of the lowlands used to fear the Ruwenzori. They thought the giant plants and strange animals that lived there were evil omens.*

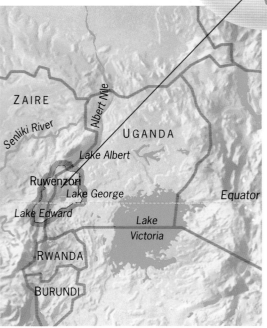

WILDLIFE OF THE RUWENZORI

Ruwenzori is a cool oasis rising from a hot, dusty plain. Below the snow on the mountain peaks is what is called the "Afro-alpine zone." Here, the plants are giants. Groundsel plants grow 6 feet (1.8 meters) high. Just below this zone, plants called tree heaths grow up to 20 feet (6 meters) high, and there are giant sedges in wet places. Strange animals of the Ruwenzori include rock hyraxes. They are small creatures like rodents – but they have hooves and they are related to aardvarks and elephants. Jackson's chameleon (*Chamaeleo jacksoni*) is a strange chameleon with a scaly skin and three horns.

Giant groundsel

Jackson's chameleon

♦ The Ruwenzori, or Mountains of the Moon, lie along the border between Uganda and Zaire. The mountains fall steeply to the Rift Valley on the western side and less steeply to the Uganda Plateau on the eastern side.

♦ The range is about 75 miles (121 kilometers) long and 30 miles (48 kilometers) wide.

♦ Snow lies on the summits all year. On the east side of the range, the snow line lies at about 14,800 feet (4,500 meters), and on the west side it lies at about 15,900 feet (4,850 meters).

♦ Unlike Africa's other high mountains, the Ruwenzori are not volcanic. They are carved from a huge block of land that was squeezed up between two faults. This rock formation is called a "horst." The Ruwenzori consist of six separate masses of rock.

♦ Some of the Ruwenzori rocks contain deposits of copper and cobalt.

▶ *Africans living in the hot lowlands at the foot of the Ruwenzori never knew snowfalls. They thought the icy mountain peaks were covered in salt.*

◀ *In temperate climates, lobelias are small garden plants, and groundsel is a little weed, but in the Ruwenzori they are the size of forest trees.*

AUSTRALIA AND THE PACIFIC

AUSTRALIA IS the smallest continent. It began as part of the ancient supercontinent, Gondwana. About 130 million years ago it broke away and began to move north. It has been wandering ever since. Geologists calculate that in 60 million years it will collide with Asia.

Most of Australia is made of very ancient rocks which have worn down into lowlands. There are young, high mountains only in the east. They were pushed up by pressure from the Pacific plate on which New Zealand lies.

The islands of the Pacific

New Zealand is a young country. It is right at the point where the Pacific plate is moving beneath the Indian plate, which carries Australia. Active volcanoes, like the 9,177-foot (2,797-meter) Mount Ruapehu on North Island, are building up the land with lava. Geysers and hot springs are other signs of volcanic activity.

"Australasia" consists of Australia, New Guinea, New Zealand, and the South Pacific islands. Many of the thousands of Pacific islands are made of coral, or are surrounded by reefs. Some are the summits of undersea

Indian Ocean

PURNULULU *p*80–81 •

NORTHERN TERRITORY

A U S T R A L I

ULURU *p*76–77 •

WESTERN AUSTRALIA

SOUTH AUSTRALIA

◄ *Australia is a continent of lowlands. Rainforest covers part of north Queensland's humid coastal plain.*

▼ *Kata Tjuta is one of the strange rock formations that rise above the hot, dry central plateaus.*

Kauai

Nihau

Oahu

Molokai

Maui

Lanai

Kahoolawe

North Pacific Ocean

Hawaii

▲ *The undersea volcanoes that form the Pacific island chain of Hawaii are, from seabed to summit, the highest mountains on Earth.*

/ GUINEA

GREAT BARRIER REEF *p78–79*

South Pacific Ocean

SLAND

TH WALES

Australian Alps

**FACTS ABOUT AUSTRALIA
AND THE PACIFIC**

♦ Australia, the smallest continent, has an area of only about 3 million square miles (8 million square kilometers).

♦ About 30 percent of Australia is desert, with less than 5 inches (127 millimeters) of rain a year; and 30 percent is scrub, with less than 20 inches (500 millimeters) of rain a year.

♦ Mount Cook on South Island, New Zealand, is Australasia's highest mountain, 12,349 feet (3,764 meters) high. The highest mountain in Australia is Mount Kosciusko, 7,316 feet (2,230 meters) high.

♦ The Pacific plate is carrying New Zealand north, so the Pacific Ocean, the world's largest ocean, is shrinking.

▼ *No one knows how many islands there are in the Pacific, but there are more than 30,000 in the South Pacific alone. These islands off Australia's east coast are called "cays." They are made of coral overlaid with sand.*

▲ Mt. Kosciusko

Tasman Sea

North Island

▲ Mt. Ruapehu

SMANIA

NEW ZEALAND

MILFORD SOUND *p82–83* •

▲ Mt. Cook

South Island

ULURU

CLOSE TO THE geographical center of Australia is the great red rock the Aborigines call Uluru. It looks huge and dramatic, rising from a dry, level plain. Little grows on Uluru. The bare rock changes color as the sun moves across the sky. At dawn it is bright, fiery red. Later it turns deep ocher, and at times it is violet.

Uluru is visible from more than 50 miles (80 kilometers) away. It is the world's most spectacular monolith (single large block of stone). The part you can see is 1,140 feet (348 meters) high and 6 miles (9 kilometers) around. But there may be twice as much rock below the ground as above it.

Uluru is made of red sandstone, a rock formed under the sea about 600 million years ago. Earth movements raised it above sea level and tilted it, so that rocks that were laid down horizontally now stand vertically.

The rock has been eroding for 60 million years. Its surface expands in the sun and contracts in the night cold until pieces flake off. Hard rock bands stand out where water and wind have worn away softer rock between them. Eroded particles have formed dunes around Uluru. In places, the natural cement that holds the sand grains together as stone has broken down, causing the rock to erode in honeycomb patterns and caves to form at its base.

Aborigines call Uluru "the place where the wind moans between sunset and dawn." They have lived around Uluru for 10,000 years. To them, it is a sacred place.

▲ *Uluru stands high above the desert. It may not rain for years, but there are rare storms. Rain running down cracks has worn deep channels in the rock's steep sides.*

WILDLIFE OF ULURU

More than 400 types of plants, 150 bird species, and about 25 mammal species live in Uluru National Park. Kangaroos and kowaris are marsupial animals (they carry their young in a pouch of skin). Marsupials feed mainly at night and sleep by day. They need very little water. The king brown snake is one of many poisonous snake species native to the desert regions of central Australia.

Red kangaroo

King brown snake

Kowari

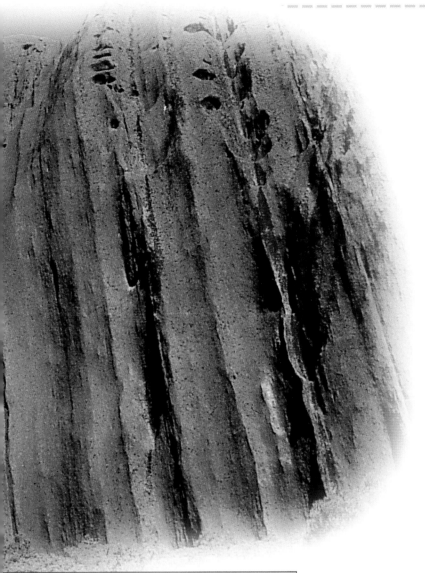

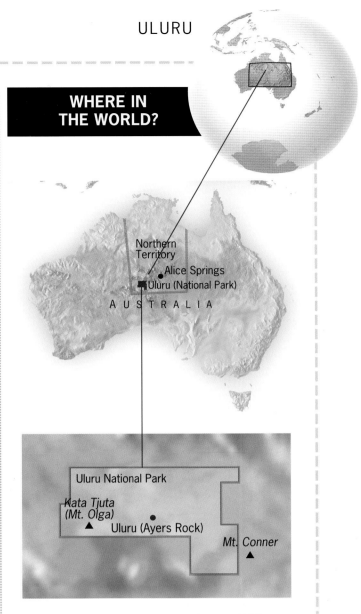

Northern Territory

Alice Springs

Uluru (National Park)

A U S T R A L I A

Uluru National Park

Kata Tjuta
(Mt. Olga)

Uluru (Ayers Rock)

Mt. Conner

◀ *From the top of Uluru, you can see for 100 miles (160 kilometers) – but at the top, the desert winds blow strongly.*

▼ *Uluru National Park was founded in 1958. Within it is Uluru and, beyond it to the west, Kata Tjuta, 36 huge, egg-shaped rocks.*

♦ Uluru is in Central Australia, 140 miles (220 kilometers) southwest of Alice Springs.

♦ Uluru is also called "Ayers Rock," and Kata Tjuta is also called "Mount Olga" or "The Olgas," meaning "many heads."

♦ Daily temperatures are 72-99°F (22-37°C) in January (summer), and 41-66°F (5-19°C) in July (winter). About 8-10 inches (200-250 millimeters) of rain falls yearly.

♦ Uluru National Park covers an area of 511 square miles (1,323 square kilometers).

THE GREAT BARRIER REEF

THE WORLD'S LARGEST coral reef forms a rampart high and strong enough to wreck ships that run aground on Australia's Queensland coast. Yet it is not one reef, but more than 3,400. And each reef is made from the hard skeletons of millions of tiny living creatures.

Corals look like plants – they are sometimes called "flower animals" – but in fact they are made by animals called polyps. Coral polyps are tiny animals without backbones. Instead, they produce a hard skeleton of calcium carbonate around them, and live inside it.

There are thousands of different coral polyps. Some live alone, but those that build reefs are called "colonial" corals. As a coral polyp grows, its circular body stretches into an oval. Then a wall of coral rock grows across the oval, and two polyps are formed. They continue dividing until hundreds of thousands of polyps, joined by their skeletons, form a reef.

Most colonial coral polyps are tiny. Their skeletons are rarely more than half an inch (12 millimeters) across. The stag's horn coral, which is one of the most common, has a skeleton less than 2 millimeters across. From above, the skeleton looks like a wheel with spokes.

As reefs have grown on the continental shelf along the Queensland coast, the sea floor beneath them has gradually sunk. Colonial corals can only live in shallow water. As those in deeper water die, others grow over them. Under the weight of new growth, the brittle branches of dead coral break and are compacted (pressed down) to form coral rock. Australia's Great Barrier Reef has been sinking and growing for many thousands of years.

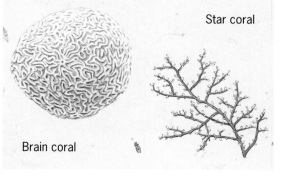

HOW A CORAL REEF GROWS

Coral polyps are animals, with stinging tentacles that paralyze their prey. They extract calcium from seawater and use it to build a stony skeleton that supports and protects their soft bodies. Coral polyps form skeletons of very varied and beautiful shapes and colours. Clusters of star-shaped star corals form boulder-shaped coral rock. Brain coral looks like a human brain.

Star coral

Brain coral

◀ Ocean waves break on the seaward side of the Great Barrier Reef. The lagoon side is a maze of small reefs. In the shallow, sheltering lagoon between the reef and the land are islands of dead coral with their own small reefs.

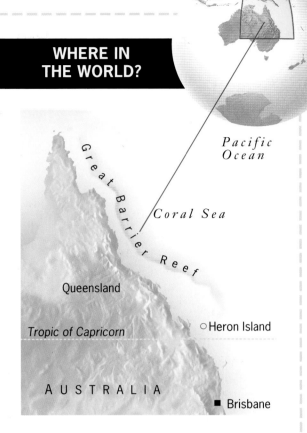

WHERE IN THE WORLD?

Pacific Ocean

Great Barrier Reef

Coral Sea

Queensland

Tropic of Capricorn ○ Heron Island

A U S T R A L I A

■ Brisbane

◆ Australia's Great Barrier Reef stretches about 1,250 miles (2,000 kilometers) from the northernmost part of Queensland to just south of the Tropic of Capricorn.

◆ On the seaward side, the reefs drop into the 6,000-foot (1,800-meter) depths of the South Pacific Ocean.

◆ The lagoon (the shallow water between reef and land) is rarely more than 30 feet (9 meters) deep. It is narrow in the north, but it widens to more than 100 miles (60 kilometers) at its southern end.

◆ There are coral reefs in the Caribbean Sea, the Red Sea, and along the coast of Kenya. But none makes as large a barrier as the Great Barrier Reef.

▲ *The treelike stag's horn coral is one of over 500 corals in the Great Barrier Reef. The reefs are home to more than 1,000 different species of fish and many other brilliantly colored living things.*

▼ *Pilot fish follow a gray reef shark.*

▲ *Heron Island in the Barrier Reef lagoon is made of dead coral. But beyond its white beach, living corals are building new reefs. Colonies of birds breed on these growing coral islands.*

PURNULULU

DOMES AND PINNACLES of striped rock separate deep gorges winding across Purnululu in Western Australia. "Purnululu" is the Aboriginal name for this strange landscape. It means "sandstone." But settlers called these hills the "Bungle Bungles." Perhaps this was their way of saying the Aboriginal word.

The rocks were formed about 300 million years ago. A shallow sea covered the region, and layers of sand and pebbles were deposited on its bed by rivers from the surrounding land. Later, earth movements pushed the land out of the sea without tilting or folding it. It became a high plateau.

Rain, rivers, and heat from the sun have broken and worn the soft rock of the plateau into strangely shaped hills separated by deep, steep-sided gorges.

WHY THE ROCKS ARE STRIPED

In January, Purnululu's dry climate is relieved by rains. For more than two months streams run through the gorges, and some of the rock layers in their sides absorb water. They remain wet for long enough for small plants to grow on their surface. After the rains they dry out. The plants die and turn black. They darken the rock until the rains make them grow again. Either side of the porous bands are layers of waterproof rock, which stand out white against the blackened layers.

▲ *Piccaninny Creek is famous for rocks shaped like beehives. They were formed by wind and rain wearing away the corners of rocks that were once rectangular blocks of stone.*

WILDLIFE OF THE NATIONAL PARK

The Bungle Bungle fan palm is one of many plants native to Purnululu, which are now rare. Dingos are dogs. They live in the desert, hunting kangaroos. Spinifex pigeons nest among clumps of the native spinifex grass. The carpet python is a snake that feeds on small mammals, such as rock rats and rock wallabies.

Dingo

Carpet python

Spinifex pigeons

WHERE IN
THE WORLD?

Darwin

Purnululu
(Bungle Bungle)
National Park

Kimberley
Plateau

Western
Australia

AUSTRALIA

Lake
Argyle

Osmond Creek

East
Kimberley

Purnululu
(Bungle Bungle)
National Park

Piccaninny
Gorge

Cathedral Gorge

Piccaninny Creek

♦ Purnululu National Park is on the northeastern side of the Kimberley Plateau in the most northerly region of Western Australia.

♦ The National Park covers 1,158 square miles (2,999 square kilometers).

♦ The gorges have steep sides. They are about 400 feet (122 meters) high.

♦ During the rainy "green season," streams flow into Lake Argyle, an artificial lake north of Purnululu.

◄ Purnululu's rock formations are very fragile. The sandstone easily crumbles. To protect its unique rocks, vegetation, and animal life, Purnululu was made a National Park in 1967.

MILFORD SOUND

ABOVE THE LAPPING WATERS of Milford Sound, bare cliff faces plunge some 3,000 feet (900 meters) to the dark water surface and drop another 1,000 feet (304 meters) below it. A "sound" is a deep inlet of the sea. The Norwegians call this a "fjord." Milford Sound is one of many fjords that bite into the northwest coast of New Zealand's South Island. This region of fjords and narrow lakes encircled by mountains is preserved by the government as Fjordland National Park.

Milford Sound is not the longest sound in Fjordland, but its waterfalls and surrounding high cliffs make it by far the most dramatic. It was dug out during the last Ice Age by glaciers more than 1 mile (1.6 kilometers) thick.

When the glacier that formed Milford Sound melted, some 10,000 years ago, seawater flooded into the deep valley it had created. As the ice retreated, it dumped a barrier of earth and rocks, called a moraine, at the mouth of the fjord. Because of this, Milford Sound is shallower at its opening to the sea than it is beneath the high mountains at its head.

Maoris – native New Zealanders – used to visit Milford Sound to look for a kind of greenstone called nephrite, which could be found there. It looks rather like jade. They used it to make axes and lucky charms, called "tiki."

▼ *Fjordland National Park is a beautiful wilderness, with snowcapped mountains, deep valleys, and glacial lakes. Milford Track is a spectacular walkers' route to Milford Sound.*

FJORDLAND WILDLIFE

Rockhopper
penguin

The coastal sounds and the outlying islands
have a rich and unusual wildlife. Penguins,
seals, and rare sea lions dive from the beaches. Bottlenose dolphins
and killer whales sometimes swim up the sounds. Blue
cod, hapuku, scorpionfish and a host of other colorful
fish live in the coastal waters. Mollymawks, and
albatrosses with 8 foot (2.5 meter) wingspans sail
above the waves and dive for fish.

Killer
whale

HOW A FJORD IS CREATED

As a glacier moves across the land, it scrapes away soil and soft rocks. It
widens and deepens valleys – often until they are deeper than the
surrounding sea. A glacier can also cut off side valleys that run into it. A cut-
off side valley is called a "hanging valley." When the
glacier melts, seawater floods into the deep
coastal valley, creating a fjord. A
river flowing through the
hanging valley becomes a
waterfall. The Stirling Falls
tumble into Milford Sound from
the mouth of a hanging valley.

Hanging
valley

Waterfall

◄ *Standing guard
more than 5,560 feet
(1,695 meters) above
the mouth of Milford
Sound is Mitre Peak
mountain. Opposite,
the Bowen Falls spout
high into the air before
plunging 520 feet
(159 meters) into the
Sound.*

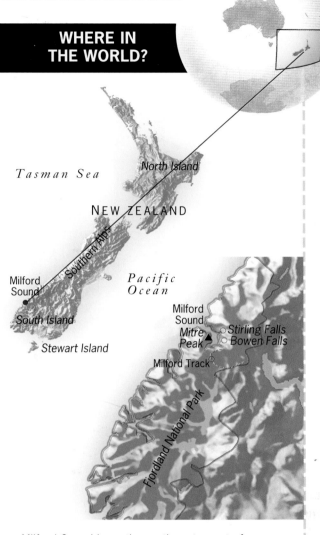

Tasman Sea

North Island

NEW ZEALAND

Southern Alps

Milford
Sound

Pacific
Ocean

South Island

Milford
Sound

Stewart Island

Mitre
Peak

Stirling Falls
Bowen Falls

Milford Track

Fjordland National Park

♦ Milford Sound is on the northwest coast of
South Island, New Zealand.

♦ The Sound is 9 miles (15 kilometers) long.
At its widest point it is 1 1/2 miles (2.5
kilometers) wide.

♦ Near the entrance, the Sound is about 400
feet (120 meters) deep. Near the head it is
950 feet (290 meters) deep.

♦ Fjordland is one of the wettest places on
Earth – about 96 inches (244 centimeters) of
rain fall of about 300 days a year.

♦ The world's longest fjord is the Nordvest
Fjord in Greenland. It is 195 miles (313
kilometers) long. Norway, Canada, and Chile
also have many fjords.

HAWAIIAN ISLANDS

THE 18 ISLANDS that form the Hawaiian chain of North Pacific islands are really the tips of mountains. In fact, the highest mountain in the world is one of the undersea mountains that form the island of Molokai. This lofty peak is called Mauna Loa, which means "Long Mountain." It rises from the Pacific Ocean floor, more than 17,000 feet (5,000 meters) to the ocean surface, then 13,677 feet (4,169 meters) above the sea. Altogether, it is more than 31,000 feet (9,000 meters) high – over 2,000 feet (600 meters) higher than Everest.

Mauna Loa and the other Hawaiian mountains are volcanoes. The islands are made of volcanic rock. There are two active volcanoes on Hawaii, the biggest and most southerly island in the chain.

Geologists have puzzled about this, for the Hawaiian islands are in the middle of the Pacific continental plate, far from where most volcanoes are found. But Hawaii lies over a hot spot in the Earth's surface. As the Pacific Plate pushes slowly over it, a new volcano erupts, to make another island. This happens once in about a million years. Sometimes, cracks appear in the volcano sides and lava flows roll out of them, down to the ocean, destroying all in their path.

▲ *Fountains of molten lava may rise more than 1,000 feet (300 meters) high. They sometimes last for several months.*

▶ *The caldera of Haleakala volcano on Maui. Hawaii's active volcanoes have large calderas, but the lava erupts from vents (cracks) inside.*

Wolf spider

Hawaiian honeycreeper

HAWAII'S UNIQUE WILDLIFE

About 1,000 kinds of flowering plants, 100 bird species, more than 1,000 types of mollusks, and about 10,000 insect and spider species are found only on the Hawaiian islands. The two active volcanoes on the island of Hawaii are now protected as Hawaii Volcanoes National Park, so ecologists hope that threatened species will reestablish themselves. The Ohia lehua forest tree, the Hawaiian goose, the wolf spider, and many others are threatened by alien species introduced by settlers.

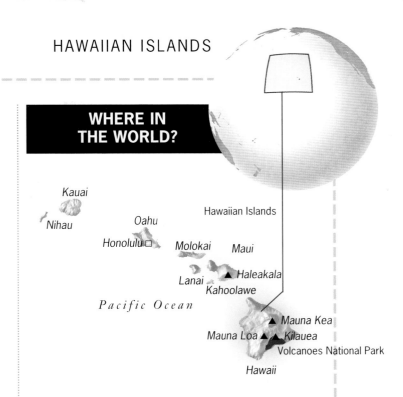

Kauai

Nihau

Oahu

Honolulu□

Molokai

Maui

Hawaiian Islands

Lanai

Haleakala

Kahoolawe

Pacific Ocean

Mauna Kea

Mauna Loa ▲ ▲ Kilauea

Volcanoes National Park

Hawaii

▲ *Lava hardens into two types of rock. This picture shows the rock called "pahoehoe," which looks like twisted ropes. The other, called "a-a," looks like clinker.*

♦ The Hawaiian Islands form a chain more than 400 miles (640 kilometers) long in the Pacific Ocean. They are nearly 3,000 miles (4,800 kilometers) from the coast of California, U.S.A., and more than 3,300 miles (5,000 kilometers) from Japan.

♦ The color of the lava as it erupts shows how hot it is. White lava is 2,700°F (1,482°C) Yellowish red lava is 2,000°F (1,093°C). Bright red lava is 1,600°F (871°C). Even when lava is cooling, the surface may break and show a red core. The temperature is about 1,000°F (537°C).

♦ Hawaii Volcanoes National Park was established in 1916. It covers 891 square kilometers (344 square miles).

♦ Hawaii and Loihi islands in the south of the chain are the youngest. They are still passing over the hot spot, so they are being enlarged by lava erupting from active volcanoes.

HOW THE ISLANDS WERE FORMED

About 70 million years ago, the Pacific plate began moving over a "hot spot" in the Earth's crust. Lava erupted through the ocean floor, forming volcanoes. These grew higher until their tops formed islands in the ocean. The volcanoes of Kauai and the northern islands died as the plate carried them past the hot spot. Meanwhile, Oahu, Maui and other islands were forming to the south.

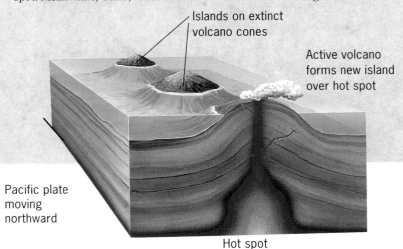

Islands on extinct volcano cones

Active volcano forms new island over hot spot

Pacific plate moving northward

Hot spot

THE POLAR REGIONS

THE ARCTIC AND THE ANTARCTIC are the icy regions at the far north and south of the globe. They are the Earth's least explored and least inhabited parts.

They are called "Polar" regions because they surround the Poles. Each Pole is one end of an imaginary line, called an "axis," around which the Earth spins. The North Pole in the Arctic and the South Pole in the Antarctic are marked by monuments in memory of the first explorers ever to reach them. Before they were explored, people thought the Polar regions were places where the Earth meets the sky.

The ends of the Earth

There is no land over the North Pole. A thick sheet of moving ice covers it. But there is land within the Arctic Circle, which is an imaginary line encircling the North Pole at 66° 32'N. It includes northernmost North America, Europe, and Asia. These are all parts of ancient, once mountainous continents which now have no volcanoes or high mountains. Large areas are covered permanently with snow, and there are some glaciers. A thick ice sheet covers Antarctica, but it is a real continent under the ice cap.

The polar winter

The Poles are dark all day in winter, which lasts for 176 days – almost 6 months. On the first day of summer, the sun rises and stays visible in the sky. For 189 days, night does not fall over the Poles.

EUROPE

ASIA

Atlan

Arctic Circle

GREENLAND (KALAALLIT NUNAAT)

Arctic Ocean

. North Pole

Bering Strait

Pacific Ocean

N

◀ *This huge iceberg has been calved from one of Greenland's ice shelves. Greenland (Kalaallit Nunaat), in the Arctic Circle, is the world's second largest island (after Australia), and it is covered with an icecap nearly 2 miles (3.25 kilometers) thick.*

FACTS ABOUT THE POLAR REGIONS

♦ In central Greenland (Kalaallit Nunaat), the average annual temperature is -27°F (-33°C).

♦ Antarctica contains 95 percent of the world's ice and snow. In winter the sea ice surrounding the continent increases to cover an area of 8,100,000 square miles (21 million square kilometers).

♦ The ice in the north and south polar regions together covers about 12 percent of the area of the world's oceans.

♦ The Polar icecaps have few permanent wildlife residents, but the Arctic Ocean and the oceans around Antarctica are rich in fish, seals, whales, and other sea creatures.

▲ *Penguins throng a glacier in Antarctica.*

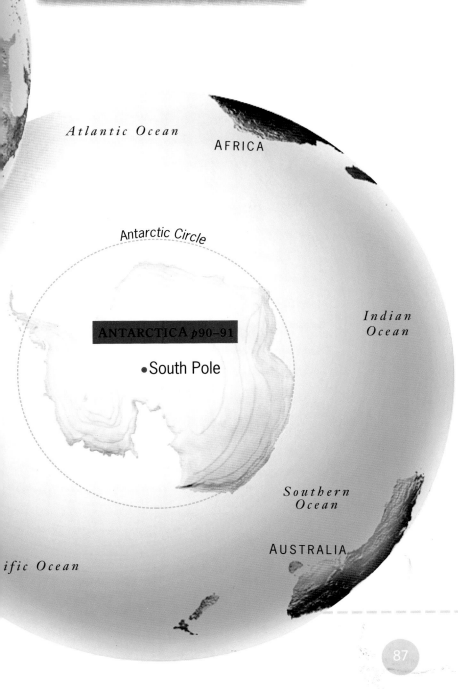

Atlantic Ocean

AFRICA

Antarctic Circle

ANTARCTICA *p90–91*

•South Pole

Indian Ocean

Southern Ocean

AUSTRALIA

ific Ocean

▲ *Icicles form on an Antarctic iceberg as it drifts north into warmer waters and melts. Thousands of huge icebergs, some more than 100 miles (160 kilometers) long, calve from the ice cliffs of Antarctica each year. They drift north and are then carried westward by the winds and currents of the Southern Ocean.*

THE ARCTIC

THE ARCTIC IS AN island of frozen ocean as big as a continent. Between the ice and the sea floor are an average 13,000 feet (4,000 meters) of the Arctic Ocean. Many of the rivers of North America and Russia flow into it, making it less salty than most other seas. Its low salinity (salt content) explains why it freezes into thick ice. Very salty water needs temperatures even lower than those of the Arctic to freeze.

The Arctic Ocean is almost surrounded by the continents of North America, Europe, and Asia. Most of its waters flow into the North Atlantic. Greenland (Kalaallit Nunaat) makes the gap through which its waters flow into and out of the Atlantic very narrow. On the other side of the world, the Arctic waters mingle with the Pacific Ocean through the Bering Strait.

Around the North Pole, the sea is frozen all year, but the ice moves with the ocean currents. It is called "pack ice" because it is floating ice which packs into a solid block in winter. In summer huge icebergs break off it. These float south, carried by the slow Atlantic current. If they reach the north Atlantic they may be a danger to ships.

At the Arctic Circle the winter is long and dark, but the sun remains hidden below the horizon for only one 24-hour period in midwinter. After that, the days gradually lengthen until, on midsummer day, the sun does not set and there is daylight for 24 hours.

Nothing grows on the Arctic ice, but lands in the Arctic Circle have a brief, brilliant summer. The upper 18 inches (0.5 meters) of soil thaw, and colorful saxifrages, geraniums, and other small plants bloom. They make food for reindeer, lemmings and other animals.

▼ *An Inuit (Eskimo) hunter waits for seal in a kayak off north-west Greenland (Kalaallit Nunaat) in the Arctic Circle.*

ARCTIC WILDLIFE

Huge numbers of birds, such as the Arctic tern, migrate to the Arctic Circle to breed during the short summer. Dragonflies, mosquitos, and many other insects emerge, so insect-eating birds are sure of catching food for their chicks. Polar bears live on icefloes and feed on fish and seals. The Arctic fox lives in burrows in the tundra regions. The narwhal, a kind of whale with a long tusk, lives in the Arctic Ocean.

Narwhal

Polar bear

RUSSIA

Arctic Ocean

North Pole

North Geomagnetic Pole

GREENLAND (Kalaallit Nunaat)

Lappland
SWEDEN
NORWAY

Atlantic Ocean

Arctic Circle

Alaska

U.S.A.

Pacific Ocean

CANADA

▲ *About 12,000 icebergs are calved annually into the Arctic Ocean. They weigh, typically, 1.5 million tons. They stand 260 feet (79 meters) above the water and 1,200 feet (366 meters) below it. Some drift as far as the Atlantic Ocean but by then they weigh only about 150,000 tons.*

♦ The Arctic Ocean covers an area of 4,700,000 square miles (12,173,000 square kilometers). It is 15,091 feet (4,600 meters) deep at its deepest point.

♦ The average annual temperature at the North Pole is -9°F (-23°C).

♦ July (summer) temperatures in the Arctic average 41°F (5°C).

♦ The minimum winter temperature over the Arctic Ocean is usually -50°F (-27°C).

♦ The annual snowfall over the Arctic is about 1.5 inches (37 millimeters), but the snowfalls become much heavier further south.

♦ At the North Pole the sea is frozen all year. But the Arctic pack ice is thinner than in the Antarctic and it moves constantly with the ocean currents.

Mid-Atlantic Ridge

GREENLAND

ICELAND

UNDER THE NORTH POLE

The northern tip of the mid-Atlantic Ridge, an undersea mountain range, rises from the seabed under the Arctic Ocean. Here, the Eurasian and the American plates are moving apart. Lava erupted by active volcanoes along the Ridge is creating new land. Two other mountain ranges cross the Arctic Ocean floor, but their volcanoes have been inactive for a very long time.

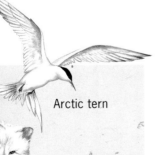

Arctic tern

Arctic fox

ANTARCTICA

ICY ANTARCTICA, the southernmost continent, has not always been so cold. Geologists have found there fossils of reptiles that lived in warmer times. They have also seen seams of coal exposed on cliff faces. Coal is formed from trees that once grew in warm climates. These coal seams must have been formed when Antarctica occupied another part of the Earth, before it drifted to its present chilly position.

Antarctica floats on one plate. It consists of old rocks that form high lands. Beneath the ice rocky plateaus rise to 13,000 feet (3,950 meters) above sea level, and mountain ranges rise almost to 17,000 feet (5,200 meters).

The Antarctic plate is a part of Gondwana, the great southern continent that once also contained the continents of South America, Africa, and Australia. About 100 million years ago, Antarctica broke away and began to drift southward.

Now, an icecap up to 1 1/4 miles (2 kilometers) thick covers the continent. It extends over the sea, forming an ice shelf that covers 1,540,000 square miles (4 million square kilometers.

▲ *Mount Erebus, overlooking McMurdo Sound, is one of several active volcanoes on Antarctica. They are the most southerly part of the "ring of fire," the ring of volcanoes encircling the Pacific Ocean.*

South Atlantic Ocean

AFRICA

Limit of icebergs

Pack ice in October

Maximum extent of pack ice

FALKLAND IS.

Antarctic Circle

SOUTH AMERICA

Indian Ocean

ANTARCTICA

○ South Pole

Pack ice in March

AUSTRALIA

South Pacific Ocean

NEW ZEALAND

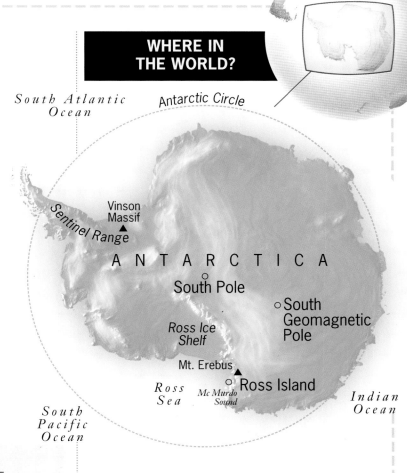

*South Atlantic
Ocean*

Antarctic Circle

Sentinel Range

Vinson
Massif ▲

A N T A R C T I C A

○ South Pole

○ South
Geomagnetic
Pole

Ross Ice
Shelf

Mt. Erebus ▲

*Ross
Sea*

○ Ross Island

Mc Murdo
Sound

*South
Pacific
Ocean*

*Indian
Ocean*

ANTARCTIC WILDLIFE

Antarctica has little wildlife. Most animals leave before winter begins. Only emperor penguins incubate their eggs through the coldest months. But the Southern Ocean teems with life, from whales and seals to fish, such as icefish, which have natural antifreeze in their blood.

Emperor penguin

Weddell seal

◄ *Antarctica is the only continent that is uninhabited by humans. Scientists often pass the winter there, but there are no permanent residents.*

♦ Antarctica's landmass covers 5.5 million square miles (14,200,000 square kilometers).

♦ The continent is almost covered with ice sheets averaging 6,560 feet (2,000 meters) thick. This is about 7 million cubic miles (29,178,824 million cubic kilometers) of ice. The depth of snow above the ice is as high as 300 feet (92 meters) in places. If this ice and snow melted, the world's major cities would be submerged by the seas.

♦ The landmass averages 7,000-7,700 feet (2,134-2,438 meters) in height. The highest mountain, the Vinson Massif in the Sentinel Range, is 16,864 feet (5,140 meters) high.

♦ The Ross Ice Shelf in southern Antarctica is almost 400 miles (650 kilometers) long, with ice cliffs more than 200 feet (60 meters) high. They are the source of many icebergs, some over 100 miles (160 kilometers) long.

GLOSSARY

A

Altiplano An area of fairly flat land between the main ranges of the Andes.

Archipelago A group of islands close to each other.

B

Basalt A dark, fine-grained, igneous rock. It erupts from fissures in volcanoes that do not erupt explosively. It can form lava fields thousands of feet or meters thick.

C

Calcium carbonate A chemical formed from the combination of three elements: calcium, carbon, and oxygen. Its chemical formula is $CaCO_3$. It is often found in a very pure form in limestones.

Caldera A huge basin-shaped depression. A caldera is caused by the destruction of a volcanic cone.

Canyon A steep-walled ravine. A canyon is cut by a river in a hot, dry area, where it does not rain often, but rainfalls are heavy. The valley is not widened by frost or other forms of erosion.

Cataract A series of small waterfalls found where a river crosses a band of hard rock.

Cave An underground tunnel. The largest natural caves are formed in limestone rocks that are eroded chemically by acid water. The tunnels may be enlarged to form huge caverns (chambers), which may be connected by vertical drops called "sink holes" or "swallow holes."

Cirque A hollow in a rock on a mountainside where a glacier begins. When the ice reaches a depth of at least 110 feet (33 meters), it cracks. The back wall of the hollow is steepened and the floor deepened by ice movement. A cirque is also called a "corrie."

Column A cylindrically shaped piece of rock. Some basalts, as they harden, crack to form polygonal columns. Columns are also formed in caves when a stalactite and a stalagmite meet.

Confluence The place where two rivers meet.

Conglomerate Rock formed by pebbles that have become cemented together naturally. The pebbles have often been carried by fast-flowing streams. Conglomerates may also be formed from accumulations of pebbles, such as those on beaches.

Cone The symmetrical pile of ash and cinders that often forms round the vent of a volcano that erupts explosively.

Continent A large landmass.

Continental drift A theory that explains the fact that the continents have moved, and are moving, slowly across the Earth's surface.

Continental shelf A gently sloping extension of a continent, covered by seawater to a depth of about 427 feet (130 meters). Beyond this is the continental slope, where the sea becomes deeper very rapidly.

Coral A kind of polyp – a tiny animal without a backbone. It extracts calcium carbonate from seawater to make itself a support in which it lives. "Coral" is also the name of its support – its bony skeleton. There are more than 6,500 different kinds of corals and their close relatives, the sea anemones. The corals that form reefs are called "colonial corals." Hundreds of thousands, joined by their bony skeletons, form the reef.

Crater The depression that surrounds the vent of a volcano. It may be several hundred feet or meters deep. It is often surrounded by steep cliffs, which form the inner part of a volcanic cone.

Crust The outer, rocky surface of the Earth. Its thickness varies between 4 and 30 miles (6 and 48 kilometers). It is thickest under the continents, where it is formed mainly of granitic rocks, and thinnest under the oceans, where it is composed mainly of basaltic rocks.

D

Delta A fan-shaped area of sediments dropped by a river as it enters the sea or a large lake.

Depression An area of lowland, completely surrounded by higher land.

Desert A very dry area. In a desert, the rainfall averages less than 5 inches (12.5 centimeters) a year. Some desert areas may not have any rain at all for many years.

Dune A ridge or small hill of sand, blown by the wind. Dunes are found mostly in deserts and by the sea. Many dunes change shape as they are moved by the wind.

E

Earthquake A movement of the Earth's surface. An earthquake is caused by slippage or other changes deep within the crust.

Equator An imaginary line round the middle of the Earth, halfway between the North and South Poles. It is 24,902 miles (40,067 kilometers) long.

Erosion The ways in which rocks on the Earth's surface are worn away, mainly by frost, ice, moving water, and wind.

Eruption The way in which lava, steam, and gases are thrown from a fissure (crack) in the Earth's crust by a volcano.

F

Fault A weakness in the Earth's crust where the rocks are torn or broken. It is caused by stresses set up by the movements of plates, or by volcanic activity.

Fissure A long, narrow crack or break in a rock surface.

Fjord A long, narrow, deep bay of the sea surrounded by high mountains.

Fold A bend in the Earth's crust due to pressure from mountain-building forces.

Fossil The remains of a plant or animal that was buried soon after it died. It was preserved usually by minerals from the water in the ground that surrounded it. Fossils are found only in sedimentary rocks.

G

Geology The study of the history of the Earth, what it is made of, how it was formed, and how it has changed.

Geyser A jet of very hot water and steam thrown as high as 197 feet (60 meters) into the air from an underground source. Geysers usually occur near areas of volcanic activity.

Glacier A river of ice.

Gorge A narrow, steep-sided valley cut by a river, usually through hard rock. Some gorges, such as Cheddar Gorge, England, are collapsed caves in limestone country.

Granite A coarse-grained igneous rock. It is formed underground from a mixture of three minerals: quartz, feldspar, and mica, which often occur as large crystals.

Gully A small, narrow valley formed by a river, but sometimes dry.

I

Ice sheet A layer of ice that covers a large area several thousand feet or meters deep.

Ice shelf The continuation of an ice sheet beyond the land. It floats on the seawater.

Irrigation Making dry, barren land fertile by supplying it with water, so that it can be used to grow crops. Wells, ditches, and canals may be dug to provide water. In some parts of the world, simple devices such as a shadouf (a bucket attached to a pole with a weight at the other end) are still used to lift water from a river and pour it onto the land.

L

Lagoon An area of shallow sea close to land. It is almost cut off from the ocean by a barrier, such as a coral reef.

Lava Molten material thrown out by a volcano or a fissure eruption. On the Earth's surface, it cools and hardens to form igneous rocks.

Limestone A rock formed from minerals, including calcium and other carbonates. It may contain the remains of sea creatures, such as corals.

M

Magma Molten rock held under great pressure underground, usually below 10 miles (16 kilometers) deep. It may harden underground to form igneous rocks, such as granite, or collect in a magma chamber, which is the reservoir for a volcano. If it erupts at the surface it is called "lava."

Massif A well-defined upland area with similar structure and geology throughout.

Meltwater The very cold water flowing from the snout of a melting glacier, ice, or a snowfield.

Monsoon Seasonal strong winds and heavy rainfall found in South East Asia and in parts of north Australia and Africa.

Moraine Heaps or ridges of rocks, pebbles, and clay that were once dropped by a glacier or an ice sheet as it melted. Unlike sediments carried and deposited by rivers, moraines contain a mixture of rock fragments of all sizes.

Mudpot A pool of bubbling hot mud, found near to areas of volcanic activity.

Mudstone A sedimentary rock.

Mud volcano A mound, usually less than 164 feet (50 meters) high. It looks like a volcano, but when it erupts it produces mud, not lava. A mud volcano is usually formed when liquid mud is forced upward to the surface during a volcanic eruption or earthquake. Mud volcanoes do not usually survive for long.

N

National Park An area of scenic or natural history interest. The plants and animals in a National Park are protected by strict regulations. The government of a country funds its National Parks.

Northern Lights Sometimes called "Aurora borealis." Bright colored lights that can be seen in the sky in the far north of the world. They are caused by interactions between the Earth's magnetic field and streams of charged particles from the Sun. Similar lights may be seen in the southern hemisphere, where they are called "Aurora australis."

P

Peninsula A narrow piece of land that stretches into the sea or a large lake.

Plain A large area of flat or rolling land without big hills or valleys.

Plate One of 7 large and 12 smaller regions of the Earth's crust that carry the continents and oceans. They are sometimes called "tectonic plates" or "continental plates." The plates float on the Earth's mantle and are moved by heat currents in it. When two plates collide, mountain ranges are pushed up. In some places, plates are being destroyed. In some mid-ocean areas, new plate material is being formed. Earthquakes and volcanoes occur wherever there is plate activity.

Plateau An area of high but fairly flat land. It usually has steep slopes on at least one of its sides.

Poles The North and South Poles are the points that are farthest north and south in the world. These are different from the magnetic poles (the places on the Earth's surface a compass needle points to). The magnetic poles are constantly changing.

R

Rainforest A forest that grows in areas of very high and nearly constant rainfall. The greatest rainforests that survive in the world today are in tropical regions in South America, Africa, Southeast Asia, and northern Australia. There are tiny remnants of temperate rainforests in the northwest U.S. and Canada.

Rapids A stretch of a river where the water flows faster because the slope of the river bed has become steeper. This is usually where the river runs over a band of hard rock. This hard rock is often exposed as boulders in the river bed. Rapids can be seen as areas of white (foamy) water, with small waterfalls.

Ravine A deep, narrow river valley, not so steep-sided as a gorge.

Reef A band of rocks near the coast which are partly uncovered at low tide. The rocks may be of any kind. Coral reefs are made of coral rock. In some parts of the world, lines of hills are called reefs. Mineral veins bearing gold or other precious metals are also called reefs in some places.

Ridge A line of steep-sided hills. These may be on land or below the oceans. Mid-oceanic ridges are hills that arise on the ocean floor where plates are forced apart by new rock formation.

Rock Solid mineral matter that forms the Earth's crust. The three main types of rocks are: **1 Igneous rocks**, made from material coming directly from the Earth's interior, such as granite and basalt. **2 Sedimentary rocks**, formed from particles eroded from other rocks and deposited somewhere else, such as sandstones and shales. **3 Metamorphic rocks**. Rocks that may have started as igneous or sedimentary rocks, but have been altered by great pressure or heat, such as slate, marble, and garnet.

S

Sandstone A coarse-grained sedimentary rock, with a grain size varying in diameter from 2 millimeters to 1/16th of a millimeter.

Scrub Coarse vegetation, usually growing in dry or semi-desert places.

Seamount An isolated, conical mountain rising at least 3,300 feet (1,000 meters) from the ocean bed, but not reaching the sea surface. Most are in the Pacific Ocean and are probably the result of volcanic action.

Sediments Grains of rock eroded and carried by wind or water, and laid down in a new place.

Shield An ancient part of a continent around which new rocks and mountain ranges have been formed more recently in the geological timescale.

Silt Fine-grained sediments, with a particle size of 1/500th to 3/50ths of a millimeter.

Slate A hard, fissile metamorphic rock ("fissile" means "can be split"). It is formed, as the result of great pressure, from fine-grained mudstones.

Source The source of a river is the place where it starts.

Spring Water flowing from the ground.

Stalactite A deposit like an icicle hanging from the roof of a cave. It is made of a calcium mineral called "calcite" that comes out of the water dripping from the cave roof. The calcium mineral was originally in the limestone in which the cave is formed.

Stalagmite A column growing up from a cave floor, made of the same material as a stalactite. It is formed when mineral-rich water drips onto the cave floor.

Supercontinent Huge landmasses that existed in the past, such as Gondwana and Pangea, which have split up to form the seven continents that exist today.

T

Taiga The Russian name for the coniferous forests that stretch around the northern continents, south of the tundra.

Travertine A light-colored form of calcium carbonate. It is dissolved in some hot spring waters and comes out of them when they flow out of the ground.

Tributary A small river that joins a larger river.

Tropics The Tropic of Cancer is the line of latitude 23.5' north of the equator. The Tropic of Capricorn is the line of latitude 23.5' south of the equator. The tropics mark the furthest points north and south where the sun is overhead at midday on June 21 and December 22 respectively. Regions between the tropics have warm climates.

Tundra A Lapp term meaning "without trees." The tundra lies north of the taiga in Europe, Asia, and North America. The subsoil is permanently frozen, but the surface unfreezes to a depth of about 20 inches (51 centimeters) in summer.

V

Vent The opening through which lavas come to the surface from a volcano.

Volcano An opening in the Earth's crust connected to an underground magma chamber. Active volcanoes may erupt at any time. Molten lava, gases, steam, and volcanic bombs are thrown from them, but not flames. Dormant volcanoes have not erupted for a long time, but may erupt again. Extinct volcanoes have not erupted for millions of years. Volcanoes are of six types, depending on how explosive their eruptions are. The least explosive produce lava flows. The most explosive produce steep-sided, cone-shaped mountains.

Volcanic bomb A small mass of liquid or semi-liquid lava thrown from a volcano. As it cools it becomes shaped like a bomb, but it does not explode when it hits the ground. Volcanic bombs may be 3 feet (1 meter) long. Volcanic material less than 4 millimeters long is called "volcanic ash."

Index

INDEX

Addison Public Library
235 N. Kennedy Drive
Addison, IL 60101-2482